T0269909

CONNECT!

DALE CARNEGIE
& ASSOCIATES

CONNECT!

How to Build
Trust-Based Relationships

MEDIA

Published 2022 by Gildan Media LLC
aka G&D Media
www.GandDmedia.com

FIRST EDITION 2022

Interior design by Meghan Day Healey of Story Horse, LLC

Library of Congress Cataloging-in-Publication Data is available upon request

ISBN: 978-1-7225-1068-8

10   9   8   7   6   5   4   3   2   1

You can make more friends in two months by becoming interested in other people than you can in two years by trying to get people interested in you.
—DALE CARNEGIE

We would like to acknowledge the following members of the Dale Carnegie team who contributed to this book:

- Joe Hart, *President & CEO*
- Christine Buscarino, *Chief Operating Officer & Chief Marketing Officer*
- Ercell Charles, *VP of Customer Transformation & Carnegie Master*
- Silvia Carvalho, *Carnegie Master, Senior Director of Training Quality, Latin America*
- Nan Drake, *Carnegie Master, Director of Training Quality Online & North America*
- Nigel Alston, *Trainer, Eastern & Central North Carolina*
- George Cantafio, *Trainer, Miami/Fort Lauderdale, FL*
- Rebecca Collier, *Global Carnegie Master*
- Grace Dagres, *Senior Trainer, Ontario, Canada*
- Andreas Iffland, *Carnegie Master, Germany*
- Robert Johnston, *Master Trainer, Delaware*
- David Kabakoff, *Trainer, Memphis, TN*
- Jayne Leedham, *Carnegie Master, United Kingdom*
- Tom Mangan, *Master Trainer, Pittsburgh, PA*

(continued)

- Laura Nortz, *Master Trainer, Cleveland, OH*
- Rena Parent, *Master Trainer, Pensacola, FL*
- Antoinette Robinson, *Trainer, Atlanta, GA*
- Jeff Shimer, *Master Trainer, Tampa Bay, FL*
- Frank Starkey, *Master Trainer, Dallas, TX*
- Jonathan Vehar, *(former) VP of Product*

CONTENTS

PART ONE

Awareness and Mindset

PART TWO

Competency and Creating Connection

FOREWORD

by Joe Hart, CEO of Dale Carnegie & Associates

Early in my career, I read *How to Win Friends and Influence People* and it impacted me profoundly. Most importantly, it helped me realize that I could be much more effective in my interactions with others if I applied the timeless and powerful principles put forth in Dale Carnegie's classic book.

For twenty-five years, I developed these skills and saw my personal and professional relationships flourish. I became very good at listening, looking people in the eye, being empathetic, and offering a friendly smile to others. And then 2020 and COVID-19 hit. Overnight, things changed for me and for all of us.

When we couldn't leave our homes, go to our places of work or even see the smiles of our friends and colleagues from behind their masks, our personal connections with other people suffered. Add to that the changes in social dynamics driven by a hyper-polarized political climate, vaccine and mask mandates, and other hot-button issues, and it's been harder than ever to know what to say to someone you're just meeting for the first time . . . or even whether or not you should shake their hand.

The good news is that the basic principles of how we create and nurture relationships has not changed, even if it looks a bit different and requires more hand sanitizer. We still need to focus on building connection, cooperating with others, and getting along. In short, we need to work our way through the rapid changes and curves that the world throws at us.

Human beings aren't wired to operate independently. Living the life of a hermit on a subsistence farm without other people around us is likely not what any of us would choose. We are social beings who create mutually beneficial relationships to survive, thrive, and enjoy life.

Think about the person who is closest to you. Perhaps a significant other, a family member, a lifelong best friend, or a mentor. And imagine if they'd never been in your life. For most of us, it's not a happy thought. The good news is that they are there for you, and you're there for them. And because of that, your life is richer and fuller. So is theirs.

This book is about helping you improve your life by creating and building stronger relationships with other people, whether it's at home or work, in-person or virtually. It offers insights that can enable you to achieve your full potential thanks to the support and friendship of others.

Dale Carnegie recognized that everyone has inherent greatness. Our work at Dale Carnegie Training is all about bringing that greatness out so that everyone can see it. Continuing his work, we change how people see themselves, so they can change how the world sees them, and that changes the impact they have on the world. It's work about which we're passionate. And it's work that no one can do alone, which is why we all need to continually build and develop connections with others.

We're excited to see what you'll bring to the world with the new connections you'll build based on what you learn in this book.

HOW TO USE THIS BOOK

Every morning, in virtually every country on the planet, Dale Carnegie trainers are preparing to share the timeless messages created by our founder Dale Carnegie. Whether we are connecting with members of the public, workers in Fortune 500 companies, or anyone in between, the lessons and skills taught have been improving and empowering people for eighty five years.

When we consider the societal changes that have happened globally since *How to Win Friends and Influence People* was originally published in 1937, it becomes apparent that the message from that book (and the training that came from it) never go out of date. They are truly timeless.

The Human Relations principles that are the foundation of our work can be applied in a variety of settings. From our homes to our places of worship, from the classroom to the boardroom, when we learn how to truly connect with one another, we can move mountains.

As you read this book, you'll discover ways to apply the information that you might not have considered before. We find ourselves making interesting connections in the most surprising places! When we focus on creating genuine connections, the entire tone of our lives become happier and more fulfilling. Brief encounters leave us with a smile and we find ourselves feeling a little less lonely in an otherwise isolating world.

Since we assume that you're reading this to somehow improve your ability to connect with others, we'd offer a few tips for interacting with this book:

1. The proven Dale Carnegie Performance Change Pathway offers some insights to set us up for success:
   • Be aware of your goals: Since this book is in your hands, we know you *want* to change. Having an emotional commitment with something at stake (e.g. success, happiness, friends, effectiveness, etc.) will ensure you take action. As you read the book, connect what you're reading to how you see yourself and what you want to accomplish.
   • Commit to experience learning: No one has all the answers. So if we're reading this to confirm what we already know, we might as well go do something else. Just like a Dale Carnegie training program is intense and can take us out of our comfort zone, this book may make some suggestions or we might make some links to the content that makes us

uncomfortable. These are the things we should pay attention to! If we think, "I don't think I could do that," or "I don't think I want to . . ." then that may be the thing that really shifts our behavior and our performance. Let's be sure to make notes, highlight, flag, dog-ear or underline those things that strike us as relevant and useful.

- Sustain the learning: When we finish the book, let's not just put it back on the shelf and go back to the old ways. No! Let's create a way to keep the learning alive! Let's commit to creating time on our schedules to make connections, find a partner who will hold us accountable to our goals (e.g. a friend, a mentor, a manager, a significant other, a relative) and check in with us periodically to see how we're doing. We may be surprised at how people around us will support us when we ask for help and demonstrate that we're willing to work to improve.

2. Make notes. Whether we're using an e-reader or a paper copy, feel free to liberally underline/highlight those parts of the book that are interesting, intriguing or useful. Let's flag those parts of the book that are relevant so that we can review them quickly. We shouldn't think of this as some pristine manuscript that we can't alter. Let's make it our own and think of it as a workbook.

3. At the end of each chapter, we should ask ourselves if we're ready to move on, or if we need to review

what we've just read. It's not a race to finish. It's about understanding and integrating the content so that we can give it a try to improve our performance.

4. Teach someone else! A great way to learn something new is to teach it to someone else. When we find something that resonates with us, let's take time to share it with someone else. Not in a formal classroom setting, but perhaps over a meal, while sharing a cup of coffee, while in the car, or when taking a walk. As we hear ourselves share, we'll make new connections.

5. Review the book again. As parts of the book become habits, we should review the entire book or at least the underlining/highlighting to see what parts we could still integrate into our practices.

6. Relate the content to our lives. As we read through the book, let's ask ourselves how we might have handled the situation, or how we might put this into practice to help achieve our connection goals.

As Dale Carnegie said, "Knowledge isn't power until it's applied." Let's apply what we learn from the pages that follow.

FIVE THINGS THIS BOOK WILL HELP YOU ACHIEVE

(that will make you a better person)

1. Become a better listener
2. Handle conflict more easily
3. Discover the secrets to trusting relationships
4. Engage with others virtually
5. Build stronger relationships

THIRTY PRINCIPLES from
How to Win Friends and Influence People
by Dale Carnegie

At the core of everything we do at Dale Carnegie Training is the foundation of the human relations principles that Dale Carnegie created many years ago. It amazes us how relevant these ideas are to modern life. In fact, if we are faced with a challenge, all we need to do is to look at these principles and see how it can improve the situation. Here are the classic principles that truly have stood the test of time.

Build Connection
BE A FRIENDLIER PERSON
1. Don't criticize, condemn, or complain.
2. Give honest, sincere appreciation.
3. Arouse in the other person an eager want.
4. Become genuinely interested in other people.
5. Smile.

6. Remember that a person's name is to that person the sweetest and most important sound in any language.
7. Be a good listener. Encourage others to talk about themselves.
8. Talk in terms of the other person's interests.
9. Make the other person feel important—and do it sincerely.

Gain Cooperation
WIN PEOPLE TO YOUR WAY OF THINKING

10. The only way to get the best of an argument is to avoid it.
11. Show respect for the other person's opinions—never say, "you're wrong."
12. If you are wrong, admit it quickly and emphatically.
13. Begin in friendly way.
14. Get the other person saying "yes, yes" immediately.
15. Let the other person do a great deal of the talking.
16. Let the other person feel the idea is his or hers.
17. Try honestly to see things from the other person's point of view.
18. Be sympathetic with the other person's ideas and desires.
19. Appeal to the nobler motives.
20. Dramatize your ideas.
21. Throw down a challenge.

Create Change
BE A LEADER

22. Begin with praise and honest appreciation.
23. Call attention to people's mistakes indirectly.

24. Talk about your own mistakes before criticizing the other person.
25. Ask questions, instead of giving direct orders.
26. Let the other person save face.
27. Praise the slightest improvements and praise every improvement. "Be hearty in your approbation and lavish in your praise."
28. Give the other person a fine reputation to live up to.
29. Use encouragement. Make the fault seem easy to correct.
30. Make the other person happy about doing the thing you suggest.

ADVICE FROM THE MASTERS

When researching this book, we interviewed several of our own subject matter experts on the topic of connection. We asked them, "If you were to give one piece of advice to someone on how to become better at connecting with others, what would it be?" Here are some of their answers.

Ercell Charles, VP of Customer Transformation & Carnegie Master

Not connecting with others can be caused by not listening, being open, respecting, appreciating, seeking the other person's point of view. Instead, we need empathetic listening, and need to be humble enough to listen. This is the basis for finding common ground.

Nigel Alston, Trainer

Connecting with others is actually based on a formula. The quality of relationships are a function of the quality and consistency of the contact over time. We all have relationships with people we've known for years, but either the quality of that contact isn't great or we don't really see them consistently. The best relationships are made when you have high quality contacts with a person, consistently, over time.

George Cantafio, Trainer

My best piece of advice is this—It's not about you. Listen more, talk less, and be yourself! If you are genuinely interested in the other person, you'll build a connection. So many people, when they meet someone new for the first time, start talking about themselves. "I'm from Florida and have three kids and love to fish." Instead, ask the other person where they live, what their family is like, and what they love to do. You can find common ground when you listen more than when you talk.

Rebecca Collier, Carnegie Master

When I was growing up, I went to thirteen different schools. I was always the new person at school, and had to learn how to connect with others pretty quickly. It's important to develop relationships and to get as much information as you can—especially when it's a different culture than you're familiar with. Expect that they will be different from you and approach it with an attitude of curiosity. Different doesn't mean bad or good—it's just different. When you approach differences with an open attitude of asking and being curious, you can build relationships much more easily.

Grace Dagres, Senior Trainer

Over the past few years, we have all been called upon to not only change, but find a way to engage in a virtual world. It's important to remember one's own mindset and attitude and see yourself as "unapologetically human." I like to call it "flaw-some." Our flaws are what make us awesome.

To make connections, we have to make every interaction about the other person. It's about finding success together. It really does go back to the Human Relations Principles. "A person's name is the sweetest sound." Ask them how to pronounce their name! "See things from the other person's point of view." Make an effort to understand the other person and where they're coming from.

Always remember, "It's not about you. It's about them."

Andreas Iffland, Carnegie Master

Mr. Carnegie wrote that we can win more friends in two months by being interested in others than we can in two years otherwise. Ninety percent of the time, we ask closed-ended questions that reflect assumptions we're making that we want confirmation on. It's the same when we ask questions that have alternatives. "Do you prefer X or Y?" You aren't leaving any room for actual conversation.

Instead, ask open-ended questions, and then build on their responses. Once you get the response to an open-ended question, you can ask "Why did that happen?" or "Tell me more about that." That's the way to make true connections with others.

Robert Johnston, Master Trainer

It all goes back to the principle "Become genuinely interested in the other person." We've all heard that a million times. But, when you look at it a little more deeply, you see why the advice is timeless. First, Dale Carnegie says "become" genuinely interested. Not "BE." There's a difference. "Be" is something that you do. "Become" is something that you are. Embedded in this advice to "become" is the assumption that we aren't already genuinely interested in the other person. It's a mindset not an action. It's an identity. "I am a person who is genuinely interested in other people."

It also says "genuinely interested." Think about what you're like when you are genuinely interested in something. We want to know more about it. We're interested to learn and ask a lot of questions and seek additional information. We need to do that with other people. Dig beneath the surface to find similarities. Get a deeper understanding of the other person. It's a lot harder to hate someone you have something in common with.

David Kabakoff, Trainer

The pandemic required many of us to wear masks. But, it's not only a physical mask that people wear. It's an emotional one, as well. In our training classes, one of the first things we do is to help people "take off" their masks. Not literally, of course. But the mask of identity that we all have that's based on the image we want to project to the world. Real transformation occurs when we let our guard down and give another person the opportunity to build trust. The true value in training doesn't come from the content. It comes from learning to take ourselves out of the equation and put the other person first in our mindset. When we find out about another person, then we can trust them.

Jayne Leedham, Carnegie Master

Somebody gave me this advice years ago. Whenever you go anywhere where there are strangers, imagine you're hosting a party. You want everyone to feel comfortable and welcome and appreciated for being there. It's not about you and what everyone thinks of you. It's a way to step outside of yourself and to focus on the other people in the room and how you can make them feel comfortable and connected with each other.

Tom Mangan, Master Trainer

My best piece of advice is, "Don't try to do it on your own." Ask for introductions to people you want to connect with. Make introductions between other people. No one knows what you're selling, for example, unless you are able to make and have connections with other people. But, it's not just about "vertical" communication. Yes, it's important to move from topic to topic in a conversation with another person. But, it's just as important to have "horizontal" communication. Stay with the topic of conversation at hand long enough to go deep. That's where you make genuine connections. We get so hung up on the transaction and what we're going to get out of the interaction. Instead, ask, "Why should I care?" Ask questions in a conversational way with the collaborative attitude that "we are problem solvers." Surround yourself with people who will mention your name.

Laura Nortz, Master Trainer

My best advice is for people to listen to understand. Find out what other people need and see if you can be of service to them in some way. By being others-focused and engaged with the other person, you are listening to find out what their values are and where the commonalities are there. Listen to find out who that person is. What's important to them, what their goals are, what are they trying to accomplish now? Not every conversation's gonna be a deep, meaningful conversation. But when you listen to understand, you connect.

Rena Parent, Master Trainer

The advice I'm going to tell you comes from a really strong-rooted belief that our inner world is more powerful than our outer world. The power within us is ultimately the power we can manifest outside of us. And because we're talking about connection, it's really the connection within. You've probably heard or seen that visual image of the tip of the iceberg. Right. We see the tip, that's the outer world, but the power of the iceberg is under. If we spend time within first, getting our mind aligned with our heart, meaning that our thoughts are coherent with our emotions, it's really making ourselves before we meet others. When we do that, we set ourselves up with an elevated probability of good connection.

Antoinette Robinson, Trainer

For someone who wants to improve their ability to connect with others, I suggest first looking into how they connect with themselves. According to Mr. Carnegie, somehow, we lose our true essence, our inner child, as we enter the adult world. This loss may be referred to as "impostor syndrome" or "covering." I assert this is a loss of connection to one's true essence.

To fit in, many of us forfeit the higher self, resulting in mediocre lives and failed relationships. If one is not making genuine connections, one should check their heart, emotional intelligence, and self-connection ability to determine whether there is an internal disconnect present.

Jeff Shimer, Master Trainer

When it comes to being better at connecting with others, you need to be thinking of developing lifelong relationships. There was a Harvard study that looked at people's relationships over an entire lifetime and they found that the key to long life, health, success, et cetera, was the strength of the person's relationships with others. It was a better predictor of longevity than cholesterol! This doesn't mean it's going to be easy. We have to invest time and concerted effort in building these lifelong relationships. But if you start out with the intent that you're going to build a relationship that lasts, and then invest time in staying connected, the outcome will be positive both for you and the other person.

Frank Starkey, Master Trainer

I got this from one of my mentors here in Dale Carnegie, John Adams. One of the things that he taught me was that Principle One from *How to Win Friends* is don't criticize, condemn, or complain. And people have a tendency to criticize, condemn and complain! One day, he asked me, "What's the opposite of criticism?" I said "Appreciation." He taught me, "No. The opposite of criticism is understanding."

Reading through these words of advice from those who teach, practice and live the wisdom of this book, we can see themes that emerge and threads that this book weaves to create connections. Before moving on, take a moment to re-read the advice from the masters and look for threads that are new and relevant to the connections you're seeking to build.

> *"Three-fourths of the people you will meet*
> *are hungering for sympathy. Give it to*
> *them and they will love you."*
> —DALE CARNEGIE

INTRODUCTION

Ernie was feeling nervous as he walked into the conference room. It had been a long time since he'd been around this many people. It wasn't a health concern on his mind—everyone had taken the proper protocols and he felt safe physically—it was the social part of it. The rules of engagement seemed to have changed since 2020 and he was unsure how to make connections with strangers. But, this was a networking meeting and that's what he was here to do.

He'd barely gotten his name tag on when someone came up to him and looked at his name tag. "Hi, Ernie. I'm Barb." Should he extend his hand for a handshake? What kinds of questions were okay to ask these days in a work setting?

She extended her hand and introduced herself. "I'm in marketing. We focus on creating synergistic opportunities between . . ."

Ernie noticed that while she was talking, her eyes were kind of scanning the room. She had a professional smile on her face and made eye contact with him, but her speech felt very practiced and unnatural. "Tell me about your business," she said.

Ernie described his company and she had an attentive look on her face—at least from what he could tell. She said all the right things and the conversation lasted long enough to be professionally acceptable. She gave Ernie her business card and then moved on to someone else.

"Well, this is what networking is, I suppose," Ernie thought as he went to get a sparkling water. "Some things never change."

Some Things Never Change, But Some Things Need to Change

At Dale Carnegie Training, we agree that some things never change. After all, the timeless principles that our founder Dale Carnegie established are still as practical and relevant today as ever.

Now that the citizens of our world have made radical shifts prompted by the global pandemic, and adjusted to virtual meetings, remote work and social distancing, the ways we used to connect with others may seem distant or even obsolete. We yearn for real connection, deep and meaningful interactions that are based on commonality instead of what we can get from one another.

The ways of "connecting" with others so that we can sell them our wares, get our own needs met, make new friends or make ourselves look good need to change. It's time to learn or re-learn how to create real connections.

The Rules of Human Engagement

One of the advantages of using Dale Carnegie's material as the foundation for this "new" way of engaging with others is that it's not really new at all.

Dale Carnegie gives us more than just principles or a process, but he gave us a system for engaging with others. In his writings, he created a series of "Human Relations Principles" that are included at the beginning of this book. These principles serve as the foundation of all of the training we do, but in particular can serve as guideposts for how to better connect with others. Here's how the principles become a system.

Connection (principles 1–9) leads to *Cooperation* (10–12) which leads to *Change* (22–30).

In other words, Connection is the foundation and the precursor to Cooperation and Change. Connection creates rapport. Lack of connection creates indifference. Cooperation creates influence. Lack of cooperation yields compliance. Change enables leadership. Lack of collaboration around change yields resistance.

In the story of Ernie and Barb, he never got the feeling of true connection with her. There was no true rapport, and as a result he felt indifferent to her. Chances are that he'd soon forget he ever met her, and if he happened upon her business card, he'd struggle to remember the interaction. We can blame a lack of connection on masks, social distancing guidelines, virtual interaction, work context, or a million other reasons. But the truth is, connection *is* possible no matter the context. We just need to know how to do it.

What Is Connection?

To connect with someone, as we are defining it here, is to have a *meaningful interaction with someone, whether it be for a few moments or a lifetime.* What does it mean to have a "meaningful" interaction with someone? In a lot of ways, connection is like beauty—we know it when we feel it. When we leave an interaction with someone and feel that warm sense of positivity—that's connection. Similarly, we know when we *aren't* connecting with another person. It's that empty feeling that feels more transactional than meaningful.

When Jonathan Vehar travels on airplanes, he usually has his headphones in his ears. Not because he's listening to music, but because he's an introvert who welcomes the opportunity to think and let new ideas come to mind. "Yet in the millions of miles I've flown on airplanes," he says, "I've made some amazing connections. Once, while flying into Indianapolis on a small plane, we experienced severe turbulence. The kind that makes you wonder if the wings will fall off. The woman sitting next to me grabbed my hand, even though we'd never spoken. It was clear to me that she was terrified. So while we held hands, I started a conversation with her, asking her about her work, her family, and her hobbies, as a way of keeping her mind off of the turbulence. We established a genuine connection that lasted for a few minutes. I've never seen or heard from her again, but I'll never forget her or our conversation."

Connections Happen Everywhere

When we think about it, the opportunity for connection happens everywhere. It's not only happening in formal settings like networking or sales meetings. It happens every day at work and in our personal lives:

• On the phone with our insurance company
• In line for coffee and with the barista
• At a family gathering with a person we don't see often
• When we encounter someone who is different from us in a visible way
• When commenting on social media
• In the break room at work
• When we work across functions or levels at work
• And more

Connection can happen naturally, or it can be strategic. It can be planned or can happen spontaneously. And it can happen whether we're face-to-face or interacting virtually.

Instacart Connection

Terry had a flat tire and decided to use the delivery service Instacart to order her groceries. Neil, her shopper, sent her a text message.

"They're out of the whole wheat hamburger buns. Is it okay to substitute soft white ones instead?"

Terry has a choice. She can reply back with a simple "yes." Or she can make a connection.

"Well, I guess that's the universe's way of telling me to get the ones I really wanted. I was trying to be healthy when I ordered the whole wheat ones."

Neil now has a choice. He can leave it be, or write back to further the connection.

"Yes, it's definitely a sign. Thank you for writing back right away."

"Of course! I imagine it's frustrating when you're standing there waiting on an answer and the person doesn't reply back." Terry then continued the connection by showing empathy for him.

"It is! But it's customers like you that make my day."

There's no "reason" why Terry and Neil made a connection that day. He wasn't doing it for the tip (she'd already pre-set it) and she wasn't doing it to get anything either. In fact, they would never meet, as his instructions were to leave the food at the door. After the transaction, the chat line would be disabled and they would never talk again.

Connections can happen anywhere and can range from the simple to the profound. They are what adds the seasoning to the stew of life. They are the things that can make their day, and make ours, and leave us smiling. And who doesn't want to smile?

Our Perspective On Connection

Dale Carnegie's perspective on connection is one of outreach. We don't wait for others to come to us, but instead we reach out to others. We do our research, ask meaningful questions that reflect a genuine interest in the other person. And then, shift from "doing" to "being." Become present to the other person and what they are saying and thinking and feeling. This is a very different mindset than waiting for the other person to stop talking so that we can talk about ourselves. When we are emotionally available and present with another person, even if it's just for a few moments, we can create a powerful connection. It's about discovering what's important to them, and about "seeing" them for who they are and what they need or want. It's based on Dale Carnegie's ninth Principle from *How to Win Friends and Influence People*, "Make the other person feel important—and do it sincerely."

Carnegie Master Nan Drake advises, "If you're actually going to go to a networking event, do your homework. For example, if you're going to an annual holiday party, find out who's going to be there. Do some research. For example, 'So and so has three kids.' That can help you better connect because it shows you're listening and paying attention to what matters to them. It takes no time at all to find someone's LinkedIn [or other social media profile] and learn some things about them." This helps you make a connection. Did you go to the same school? Share an interest in the same volunteer causes? Live in the same city? Obtain a similar certification? Follow the same people? These little things can start a great conversation and spark a powerful connection. Between friends, colleagues, and the internet, there is no excuse not to find out about people.

Commonality from Difference

Does this mean that it's easy? That there are no challenges to connecting with different people? Of course not. In our modern world, it's become normalized to have conflict with those who are different from us. This can make some people skeptical and suspicious when we reach out to them for connection. "What do you want from me?" can be a response. "I'm not going to change for you."

Yet, those are the very situations where connection matters most. True, genuine connection can create commonality from difference. And once that is done, conflict decreases. We may not agree with the other person, but we can step inside their world for a while. And understand their perspective, and maybe change our own, or at least understand the true source of disagreement.

The truth is, it's easier to change ourselves than our circumstances. And, we can change our circumstances by changing ourselves.

How This Book Is Structured

Connect! is divided into two parts. Part One deals with the internal components of connection—our Awareness and Mindset. Part Two deals with the interpersonal components—Skills and Reaching Out. Combined, these lead to Connection.

Awareness and Mindset + Skills and Reaching Out
= Connection

Key Takeaways

- Dale Carnegie Training has been in the connection business since 1912.
- **Connection** (principles 1–9) leads to **Cooperation** (10–12) which leads to **Change** (22–30)
- Connection creates rapport. Lack of connection creates indifference
- Connecting means discovering people's core desires— what's important to them It's something we do all the time, not just to get something
- Types of connections
    1. Work/Personal
    2. Live/online
    3. People like us/people different from us
    4. Natural/strategic
- Real connection is not transactional. It's based on Principle #9: make the other person feel important— and do it sincerely.
- Dale Carnegie's perspective on Connecting: Don't wait for them to come to you
- It's not about doing, it's about "being:" I'm available for you

• It's easier to change ourselves than our circumstances, and we can change our circumstances by changing ourselves.

> "It's not enough to understand the principles, you have to apply them. If it's learning how to deal with stress and worry, you have to get out there and deal with it. If you want to learn how to speak, you have to stand up and speak. If you want to swim, you have to jump in the water. You can't swim without getting in the water, and you can't connect without being with other people."
> —NIGEL ALSTON

Part One

Awareness and Mindset

To change performance, you have to change emotions and behavior first

It's been said that all change starts from within. That's why Part One of *Connect!* starts by looking at the factors that lie within each of us. Connection comes from both awareness and mindset. When we become aware of our conscious and unconscious thoughts about those who are similar to and different from us, when we unfurl our natural affinities and our self-imposed limitations, when we discover the value not just in what we share but also where we are unique, and when we develop the ability to shift frames and filters, then we can be in the right mindset to form deep and meaningful connections.

1: PEOPLE ARE DIFFERENT
(But Also the Same)

Thanksgiving was always Ernie's favorite holiday. Not just because he loved his Aunt Vera's apple pie and his mom's sausage stuffing. Ernie loved Thanksgiving because it gave him a chance to connect with family members that he often only got to see once a year or so. Sure, his family was a little crazy. But whose isn't?

As Ernie pulled into the driveway of his cousin Eddie's house, he could see that several family members were already there. He couldn't help but wonder if things would be different this year. Would it feel the same? Or would it be harder to tolerate the people with whom he doesn't get along?

What Difference Can Connecting with Others Make?

Research shows that 71 percent of people turn to family and friends in times of stress.* Humans are social beings

---

* https://www.mhanational.org/connect-others

who are biologically driven to get emotional and physical needs met through relationships with others.

Research points to the benefits of social connection:

- Increased happiness. In several compelling studies, a key difference between very happy people and less-happy people was good relationships. This is true in the workplace and our personal lives.
- Better health. Loneliness was associated with a higher risk of high blood pressure in a recent study of older people.
- A longer life. A nine-year study found that people with strong social and community ties were two to three times less likely to die.

What can that look like in our own daily lives? Connection can take many forms, from concrete help to a good laugh, to support and emotional validation.

"Can you pick my kids up from school today? I'm stuck in traffic."

"I am so sorry you're having such a tough time right now."

"I know it's hard to have a sleepless newborn. It won't last forever, and hang in there in the meantime. You can do this!"

"What if you and Lesley planned a weekly date night with just the two of you?"

"I thought I was the only one who dreamed of just getting on a plane and flying somewhere new the same day!"

Differences and Similarities

Most of us have encountered (or even had) siblings who were completely different from each other. Even identical twins, who share the same DNA, can be different! Actor Rami Malek, for example, is outgoing and extroverted, winning awards and the red carpet spotlight. His twin brother Sami Malek doesn't share these qualities, but prefers to stay away from the attention his brother seeks. Instead, Sami chose a career in academia and spends his days teaching.

How can people be so different from each other? The answer lies in our similarities. Even though we may express them differently, human beings have a core set of common interpersonal needs.

Three Basic Needs

1. How much do we share? American Psychologist William Schutz spent his career studying interpersonal needs. His insights about these needs emerged from his early work studying sailors serving on submarines as a way to improve performance. We can imagine that a submarine is a place where people have to work well together and find it difficult to get away from each other during a three to six month deployment. Schutz stated that the need for **affection or openness** is core to all humans. (Appreciation is another form of affection.) Everyone needs to be appreciated and recognized, but we have individual differences on how we get those needs met and how much of it we want. For example, some of us demonstrate openness or affection by sharing what's happening for us to many people, much of the time. Others are more likely to play their cards close to the vest. Some people want to know what's happening with others, while others are less interested. There's no proper formula and it's important to understand that people have different needs to share and to hear from others.

2. Who is in charge? In addition to affection/openness, people also have a need for control. **Control** is the ability to influence people or events. As with affection, there are also individual differences in how we perceive control. Some of us are more likely to take control of a situation, and are comfortable doing so. Others are less interested in taking control, and are fine in a situation where things seem a bit chaotic. Similarly, some of us want others to tell us what to do, while others are not as willing to let people issue directions. Again, there's no right answer, and it's helpful to understand that people are driven by their interpersonal needs and it shapes their interactions with others.

3. Who is in our "inner circle?" Finally, Schutz says that **belonging** is a basic human need. And, like the other two needs, he also says that this exists on a continuum. People have different needs for belonging and those needs can change depending on different things. Some people want more belonging and others might want less. We may want to invite everyone we know to our birthday party. Or maybe we just want a couple of close friends. Similarly, if our neighbor is having a party, do we feel disappointed that we didn't get an invitation? Or do we breathe a sigh of relief?

These three needs of affection, control, and belonging aren't static needs, but are dependent on context. In one context, a person might have a high need for control but have a lesser need for control in another environment. One example might be the manager who insists on daily updates from her team, but doesn't have a preference for where her family goes on vacation every year.

When you look at these ideas as a whole, that we have needs of affection, control, and belonging, and that within those needs there are individual differences in how we get those needs met, and then add on the idea that people can be different in different environments, we begin to see how important communication is to being able to connect with each other. We all want to have people in our "circle," and be in other people's "circle," but to different levels. And we want to be open and have others be open with us, but at different levels (some people a lot, and some people very few).

Applied Understanding

"It's so good to see you, Ernie," said uncle Eddie. "Come on in. Your cousins and Aunt Vera are in the TV room."

Ernie could hear his cousin Peter before he even got in the house. He was talking about religion, as usual. Peter was the person at every party who shared

his opinions with as many people as he could corner.
Ernie didn't agree with Peter politically or in terms of
religion, and used to just ignore his ranting. But this
year, it felt more annoying than usual.

He decided to head over to the couch and sit next
to his niece Avery. She was definitely someone with a
low expressed need for belonging and openness. When
she was younger, Ernie could often find her off in a
corner somewhere reading. Now that she was a young
adult, she looked as awkward as ever, and just sat on
the couch looking at her phone. "Hey Avery!" he said,
as he sat down next to her.

Avery's eyes warmed as she saw Ernie. She was
likely to be relieved that he came and sat next to her
before Peter did. "Hi Uncle Ernie. It's been awhile."

As they sat and caught up on each other's lives,
Ernie's Aunt Vera came into the room with an
announcement. "I have some bad news, everyone. The
oven broke and the turkey has been sitting in it, raw,
for three hours. There's no turkey for dinner!"

Chaos ensued, as Vera's husband Andrew began
trying to place blame. "How did you not notice it
wasn't on? Couldn't you smell that it wasn't cooking?"

"How can I smell nothing? There was nothing to
smell!" Vera said. "I turned it on! You should have
checked it last week!"

"All right, all right," said Peter, trying to assert control over the situation. "We have three choices. We can
borrow the neighbor's oven and wait to eat later. We
can just eat the side dishes. Or we can go to a restau-

rant that's serving a full Thanksgiving dinner. I think we should . . ."

"What a control freak," Avery muttered to Ernie. "It's just a turkey."

Peter was definitely the kind of person who liked to control things, and the shifting of blame was Vera demonstrating her lack of interest in being controlled. Ernie chuckled and replied to Avery, "They may be freaks, but they're our freaks."

There's No Best Way

One important thing to note is that while some of the language around the different types of needs around affection/openness, control and belonging might indicate that there is one "ideal" way to be, we believe that every tendency has worth and value. An important part of connecting with others is accepting and understanding that others are different from us, and that's okay.

How can we apply these ideas to the ways we connect with others? Let's take a look at the basic human needs and the individual differences and go through them for insight into how people with these tendencies might receive connection.

Affection

People with low demonstrated desire for affection/openness are likely to be hesitant to share much in terms of personal information or stories. To connect with someone with this tendency, it's important to mirror the volume of information and openness that the other person is providing. Don't "overshare!" Keep the conversation focused on their interests and about what they're comfortable talking.

People with a high demonstrated desire for affection and openness love engaging with people, telling their stories, and receiving recognition from others. When engaging with someone like this, listening and asking questions about their experience and feeling is the key to connection.

Regardless of whether they express a high, medium or low preference, follow their lead. Be sensitive to cues that they want you to engage more and when they want to retreat from the conversation. You may need to dial up or dial down your own preferences in order to meet their needs.

Control

People who demonstrate the need to control a situation are people whose tendency is to be self-directed. They are the ones to take personal responsibility for both successes and failures, and can be quite hard on themselves when things don't turn out as planned. The area for connection, here, is recognition of that. Commenting and identifying areas where their actions led to positive outcomes ("That was a great talk you gave—everyone loved it!") and showing empathy when things don't go well ("It can be really hard when there are technical difficulties during a presentation, but you did a great job of keeping your cool!") are ways to connect with this tendency.

For those people not likely to demonstrate a desire to control a situation, we need to treat them differently. To connect with a person with this tendency, focus your conversation on that person's feeling about the situation and your common experience of it ("It really was lucky that you weren't late to the meeting. I love it when I find parking right away like that." "I'm so sorry your dog ran away when the gardener left the gate open. You must have been terrified!") Avoid pointing out the person's responsibility in the outcome ("Maybe you should have checked the gate after the gardener left?"). The point is to connect with them, not correct them.

Regardless of their demonstrated need for control, ask questions and mirror them (authentically, of course) to step inside their world and share experiences of things that are both within our control and not. Again, their preferences may not be the same as yours, but by adjusting how you normally operate to meet their needs, you may improve the connection. Dale Carnegie's principle #18 applies: "Be sympathetic with the other person's ideas and desires."

Belonging

People who demonstrate a lower preference for inviting others in are likely to be more comfortable one-on-one or in smaller groups. To connect with someone like this, first of all, look for them! They might be the person at the buffet table or off to the side just taking it all in. Understand that they may be awkward at first in conversation, but with genuine interest on your part, they can be drawn out.

Those who want to include many people in most situations may well be the one who is the life of the party! You can hear them inviting people in, checking in with everyone and ensuring everyone makes a contribution to the discussion. To make a genuine connection with a person who has this it's important to get beneath the social veneer and discover what really matters to them.

As always, it's important to recognize how much belonging they demonstrate, and recognize that this may be different than what they want. Steve regularly invited people to his house to watch football games and grill food outside. Yet when he was invited to his friends' parties, he was always a no-show. We should not take that sort of behavior personally. Rather we should respect this as what people need and adjust our behaviors accordingly.

Be Authentic

At the core of it all is the idea of authenticity. You'll read this idea time and time again throughout this book. We aren't connecting with others so that we can get something from them. It's not transactional in that way. We're not asking the barista how his day is so that we can get an extra pump of syrup in our coffee. We're asking him how his day is so that we can actually experience an authentic connection with another person. It's about being the kind of person who is genuinely interested in other people. And possibly making their day better. And ours too.

It goes both ways, though. We need to be willing to not just enter other people's worlds, we also need to let people into ours. If we go deep, they might too. Of course this doesn't mean we get into our whole life story when someone asks how we're doing today. But it does mean that we have to be willing to go first. "A greeting is something we do, not something we should expect." Until we're willing to share ourselves (regardless of our preference for affection/ openness), we will not make meaningful connections.

Essentially, when we're making connections, we're paying attention to four key things:

• What do we have in common?—Nothing bridges a gap between two people faster than discovering they have similar friends, backgrounds, experiences, interests, hobbies, passions. Part of the task of connecting is finding those similarities to create common ground. Laura, who lives in North Carolina, was teaching an online course with participants from Taiwan. Truett, one of the participants, asked if she knew Cam since they both worked in the same place. She did, and Truett and Laura made a solid connection.

• What is interesting about the other person? When we engage a person by having them talk about what is interesting to them, it creates a great connection. Aubrey Percy found herself at a dinner gathering sitting next to Lee, someone who was not engaged in the conversation. Lee didn't ask questions and didn't seem to be interested in anything. Somehow the conversation turned to brewing beer, and Lee spent the next hour engrossed in helping Aubrey understand the process and why it was so exciting! The two bonded over Lee's interest, and Aubrey forged a connection with someone who had a very, very small "inner circle."

• What motivates them? We sometimes assume that what motivates us motivates everyone. And people are different! When we can uncover what someone is motivated by, or what inspires them, we can find a way to connect with them at a deep level. Samir assumed that the members of his team were motivated by the same thing he was, and regularly referenced this in communications. He eventually found out that they were on the team for very different reasons than he was. He shifted the focus of his communications to reflect *their* interests, not his.

• What do they value? All of us have different values, and even two people doing the same job may be doing it for very different reasons. One may value the opportunity to improve the organization, and one may value the opportunity to make an impact. Or value the freedom the job creates. Or financial security. When we understand what someone values, we understand who they really are, and this is a firm foundation for a connection.

Visualize Your Best Move

Master Trainer Rena Parent says, "My husband's a former NHL hockey player and my two boys are high level hockey players and when they start to think about their inner connection of what they want to achieve and to think about what it should look like, it's about starting with the mind. Even when they're not on the ice—your mind and heart is more powerful than any of that. You need to visualize your best move. What could be your best move? You need to go inside yourself, live that as if it's already happened. And do that every single day when you go to bed, and that's exactly what the most successful athletes do. They are visualizing themselves winning."

Meanwhile, in the next chapter, we'll take a look in our collective mirrors and identify the self-imposed limitations to Connecting.

Key Takeaways

- The benefits of social connection are:
    —Increased happiness
    —Better health
    —A longer life
- The need for affection, control, and belonging is core to all humans.
    —Affection: How much do we share?
    —Control: Who is in charge?
    —Belonging: Who is in our "inner circle?"
- These three needs of affection, control, and belonging aren't static needs, but are dependent on context.
- Sometimes we need to dial-up or dial-down our own expression of those three needs
- An important part of connecting with others is accepting and understanding that there are others different from us, and that's okay.
- Essentially, when we're making connections, we're paying attention to four key things: commonality, what's interesting about the other person, what motivates them, and what they value.

"Do you know the most important trait a leader can have? It is not executive ability; it is not a great mentality; it is not kindliness, nor courage nor a sense of humor, though each of these is of tremendous importance. In my opinion, it is the ability to make friends, which boiled down means the ability to see the best in the other person."

—DALE CARNEGIE.

2: OVERCOMING SELF-IMPOSED LIMITATIONS

Ernie was standing outside on the patio break room at work trying very hard not to say something he might regret. Earlier today, his boss called him into her office today for his quarterly performance review and had given him some feedback that was really hard for him to hear. It took all of his emotional maturity to not argue with her right then and there. "She has no idea what it's like out there in the field anymore," he thought. "She's been behind that desk for more than five years. A lot has changed! I can't just walk into the clients' offices and demand to talk to the CMO. It doesn't work like that."

This isn't the first time Ernie received feedback he didn't agree with. Over time he'd learned to not say anything in the heat of the moment, but to excuse himself and calm down first. After a few minutes, Ernie

felt his blood pressure lowering. "Okay, is there any
truth to what she said? Am I holding myself back by
not approaching senior management with my ideas? Is
this a blind spot of mine?"

Have you ever been in a room with others whom you
felt were more successful than you and felt intimidated
or experienced "imposter syndrome?" Trainer Antoinette
Robinson has, and talks about how to overcome these
self-imposed limitations.

"There I was, updating my Dale Carnegie certification.
I was beyond nervous and wondering if being a Certified
Dale Carnegie Trainer is the right step for me. While sitting
among some of the best and brightest in Dale Carnegie, I
realized my inner critic was quite busy informing me, 'You
can't do this. . . .' Could I really coach high-potential individuals into their next stage of greatness? Are my credentials
good enough? A flood of doubt rushed through my mind,
and I noticed that I began to agree with my inner critic.

"Agreeing with the inner critic, a Carnegie Master
called on me to coach an executive in the room. I thought
to myself, 'Are you serious?' Somewhere between leaving
my seat, walking to the front of the training room, and
wondering if I should excuse myself to pretend like I am
going to the restroom and go home, a spark happened. I
realized that I had disconnected from my higher self, my
true essence.

"I began to recall all the leaders who have graced my life
and poured their genius into me; I thought about the count-
less times I led successful endeavors. I also thought those

who would come after me needed me to stay connected with my true essence and advance humanity. Needless to say, my higher self won, and seven years after that event, I am still a proud Certified Dale Carnegie Trainer.

"In conclusion, I borrow a phrase from the cyber world, 'Check the connection . . .' Often the disconnect is internal and not external."

How did this Carnegie Master spot something in Antoinette that she hadn't seen in herself? The answer lies in the Johari Window.

The Johari Window

We are often unaware of how others perceive us, how we present ourselves to others, and even how well we know ourselves. The Johari Window is a model to help us become self-aware, or more open. It was invented by Psychologists Joseph Luft and Harry Ingham who created this model because they understood that people don't have complete self-awareness, and that the lack of it can affect one's life.

	Known to you	Unknown to you
Known by others	**OPEN**	**BLIND SPOT**
Unknown by others	**HIDDEN**	**UNKNOWN**

There are four quadrants in the window: Open, Hidden, Blind and Unknown. Let's explore this model, or framework for increasing self-awareness, in more detail, as it relates to connecting with other people.

Open

The Open quadrant are those areas that are known to ourselves and to others. We might have family photos in the office or season seats to the Lakers. Everyone, including us, might be aware that we tend to be late to meetings or are really good with Microsoft Office. These are things about us that we are aware of, and others are too.

Hidden

The Hidden quadrant contains those areas that we know, but that we keep hidden from others. If we have been having financial difficulties and had to declare bankruptcy, for example, we may not want others to know about that. Challenges with a spouse or kids, or even that we've been looking for another job might be something that we choose to keep hidden. Hidden items don't necessarily have to be bad—they can be our strengths, too. We might not want everyone to know that we are great at bartending because then everyone will ask us to make drinks at parties from then on. Or we may hide professional strengths because we don't want to do them any more or get pigeon-holed into having to be the one who "always" facilitates meetings. Hidden things are things that we are aware of, but others aren't.

Blind Spots

Blind Spots are things that are known to others but not to us. Maybe we are a terrible singer, although we think we're great. Sometimes people who have pets aren't aware that their house smells like a cat litter box or like wet dog hair. Others are aware of it, but we aren't.

When Ernie's boss called him into her office, she was explaining to him that she felt he was selling himself short by not taking his good ideas higher up in their client organizations. She felt he had a blind spot about his own talent.

The truth is, everyone has blind spots, and they can affect the way we interact with people without even knowing it—even though we may be well-meaning. There is more on this, including a discussion of unconscious bias later on in the book.

Unknown

The final quadrant of the Johari Window is the Unknown quadrant. This is where there are things that neither we nor others are aware of. Would we enjoy hang-gliding? No one knows if we've never tried. Could we happily live on the shore of a remote lake? Would we be happy working for a much larger company? Assuming we haven't yet done it, it's unknown.

It's in the Unknown and Blind Spots quadrants where there are opportunities for communication! The more curious we are about others and the more we invite authentic connection in, the more we are able to discover things about ourselves we didn't know (and maybe help them discover things they didn't know as well!).

Identifying Blind Spots

As we wrote about in a previous book in this series, *Lead!*, blind spots can be the death of effective leadership. Dale Carnegie Training's research identified four core areas where we can be unaware of our impact. These are things that we may think we are doing well, but in reality are not.

1. Praise and appreciation. Most people say they don't get enough feedback and especially praise and appreciation. And most of us realize we don't give nearly enough.

2. Admit when we are wrong. Sometimes we focus too much on why we did it, or covering it up, when really what's needed is for us to emphatically admit that we goofed and then work on correcting it.

3. Listen, respect, and value others' opinions. We need to actively seek it out and believe it, rather than discount it because it may be different from what we believe.

4. Employees need to be able to trust leaders to be honest with themselves and others. While there are times that leaders can't share information, the more transparent and honest we are, the more trust and loyalty we build in our teams.

These four items are relevant to everyone, even if we aren't in a leadership role at work, since having an awareness of these blind spots may help all of us better see the gap between our actual behavior and our desired behavior. When we work to identify blind spots in these four areas and learn to overcome them on a personal level, it can help us form more meaningful connections with others.

Jonathan Vehar was a new trainer when his colleague Blair Miller—who happens to be a master at making connections, as you'll see later in this book—gave him the feedback to take time before the program and during breaks to connect with the participants in the training program. "Why should I bother? I'm never going to see them again," Jonathan responded. Blair pointed out that the personal connection is the foundation that allows people to be willing to let us help them and to be vulnerable enough to try something different. "Without connection," Blair said, "you can't be effective at training, leading, guiding, coaching, or anything else that involves people."

When it comes to evaluating the impact of our own behavior, keep these tips in mind:

- Assume that we are not objective when assessing our own capabilities. That means we need help. There are a variety of 360-degree feedback tools available that can provide insight into the perceptions of those with whom you work.

- Prepare yourself for feedback. It can be difficult to set egos aside, and many people benefit from learning adaptive techniques that help them approach and accept feedback constructively. At the very least, commit to not interrupting the feedback, and/or only asking questions to help you understand the feedback.

- Appreciate the intent. While getting feedback that reveals blind spots can be uncomfortable, remember that it's also difficult to give constructive feedback. Chances are, those providing it are trying to help. There's an old saying that says, "Feedback is a gift." Sometimes we want that feedback to come with a receipt so that we can return it, but it's still a gift that requires the other person to be interested enough to notice, the time to craft, and the courage to deliver it.

- Disrupt routines. We are blind to the things around us when we become set in our own ways and fall into routines regarding how we engage others, including reacting to issues, running meetings or coaching our employees.

- Just do it. Given the importance of these leadership behaviors, there's no downside to simply taking action to become even better at them. The simple act of learning can also encourage greater self-insight, which means there's twofold benefit to taking action: becoming aware of and simultaneously working to improve one's performance of these crucial behaviors for motivating employees.

"The truth will set you free.
But first it may make you angry."

Blair's feedback caused Jonathan to get angry. But he also recognized that Blair was trying to help Jonathan be more effective. Once this sunk in, they were able to work together to help Jonathan raise his game.

We can never completely eliminate our blind spots; they are part of human nature. But through candid self-reflection combined with focused effort, we can safely steer ourselves toward becoming the exceptional leaders we want to be.

With self-awareness, adopt what is known as a "learner's mind." Be open and curious, be okay with making mistakes and being wrong. Even if we strive to have impeccably high standards, we must leave our ego at the door.

Self Examination

In order to fully utilize the lower half of the Johari Window, we have to become familiar with the practice of self-examination. It's easy to know what we already know about ourselves. The practice of self-disclosure in things that are Hidden is a powerful tool in connecting with others.

Feedback

In order to fully utilize the left half of the Johari Window, we have to become comfortable with feedback. There's no other way to identify blind spots than to ask someone we trust. Asking for feedback and then being open to receive it is another powerful tool in connecting with others.

When we are committed to continuous learning and growth, we find ways to overcome our discomfort with disclosing more of what we know about ourselves and are more open to seeing ourselves from the perspective of others, such as through inviting feedback.

We're not going to love everyone, and not everyone's going to love us. But we can all appreciate each other and respect our dignity.

Relationship Mapping

One of the exercises we do in our Dale Carnegie programs is called Relationship Mapping. The intent is to look at the nature of the relationships we have in our lives and the roles we have in them. The process can be life changing. Carnegie Master Andreas Iffland shares how the process allowed him to see some important areas for change.

"In the training, we build a relationship map. As I was filling it out, I realized that all of the people who were together with me were more or less forced to be there. Co-workers. Family. I started to wonder, 'Who are my friends?' I was thirty-five years old at that point and realized that I had no real friends. The trainer then introduced the Dale Carnegie principles, and I started to see that I was overconfident. I'd been wanting to show others how good I am, how bad they are, and make that gap as big as possible. But from the training I realized that it was no way to live and so I started changing things. Treating people differently, giving honest appreciation, becoming more humble, learning from others, being interested in them, admitting mistakes. These were things I never did before and I started doing them. And you know what? It worked. Today, I'm a trainer. I'm one of the Carnegie Masters. I'm developing trainers globally. When I saw what had changed—how I had changed from these training sessions, I knew I wanted to help others. Over the years I've had difficult participants in the course. Yet I can honestly say that there were only maybe two or three people who were as bad as I was. Everyone can change. If I could change, anyone can change."

How to Do a Relationship Map

Who are the people we can trust to offer feedback and help us see our blind spots? One useful tool to answer this question is the Relationship Map. To create one, get a piece of paper and write "Me" in the center of it with a circle around it. From that, draw lines outward that connect to the names of people who are in the following roles in our lives.

- Personal relationships
- Suppliers
- Professional Associates
- Who I report to
- Who reports to me
- Community
- Peers
- Customers/clients

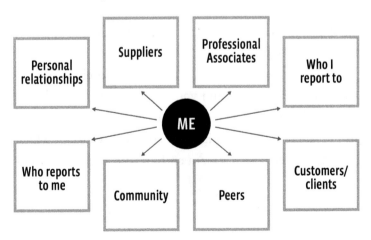

Put a star or an asterisk next to the names of those people whom we might feel comfortable asking for feedback. It's important to choose people who won't only "tell us what we want to hear," but will also be a safe and trusted person. We'll use this concept of Relationship Mapping in other exercises throughout the book.

There's a section in a later chapter on how to handle feedback you've received, as well as what to do when someone asks us to offer feedback.

The Little Realized Secret of Success

There's one "secret" of success that underlies everything we've talked about in this chapter—enthusiasm. Enthusiasm is often misunderstood as "cheerleader" or a "rah rah" behavior. Instead, enthusiasm is a mindset that we bring to connecting with others. It's when we honestly look forward to communicating and having interactions with others. We're open to what they have to say and are enthusiastic about putting our own obstacles aside and stepping into another person's world for a while. Sometimes, of course, that enthusiasm can be hard to find.

Rena Parent tells us the best way to develop enthusiasm. "Act enthusiastic and you will be enthusiastic. These are Mr. Carnegie's words which mean that you are the creator of the narrative. Let it be one that is a win-win, which ultimately means that if I am enthusiastic, you'll be enthusiastic."

ʗ   ʗ   ʗ

Excerpted from *The Little Recognized Secret of Success** by Dale Carnegie

Enthusiasm Worked Miracles For Me

I regret to say that I did not inherit any great intelligence from my ancestors, but I did develop a superior enthusiasm from my mother. Is enthusiasm important in selling? Yes, genuine, heartfelt enthusiasm is one of the most potent forces of success in almost any undertaking

Charles Schwab—a man who was paid a salary of $1,000,000 a year—told me that the secret of his success was enthusiasm. He declared that a person can succeed at almost anything for which he or she has unlimited enthusiasm.

I once interviewed Frederick Williamson on a radio program. He was, at that time, president of the New York Central Railway. When I asked for his recipe for success, he said: "the longer I live, the more certain that I am that enthusiasm is a little recognized secret of success. The difference in actual skill and ability and intelligence between those who succeed and those who fail is usually neither wide nor striking. But if two people are nearly equally matched, the one who is enthusiastic will find the scales tipped in his or her favor. And someone of second-rate ability with enthusiasm will often outstrip one of first-rate ability without enthusiasm."

---

* ©2022 Dale Carnegie & Associates, Inc.

"Emotional Drive" Is What Counts

I once heard a famous psychologist, in discussing army aptitude tests, remark that IQ tests have one important shortcoming. They fail to measure "emotional drive." According to IQ tests, a person with a low score is usually rated as fit for only menial jobs, whereas a high score is considered practically a guarantee of success. You and I know how misleading that is. I have seen people with low IQs suddenly "set on fire" by a new idea or a new line of work. It gives them "emotional drive," which sends them on to great success. And I have seen people with high IQs fail miserably.

When Mark Twain was asked for the reason for his success, he replied: "I was born excited."

William Lyon Phelps, one of the most popular teachers in the history of Yale, told me almost the same thing. Professor Phelps even wrote a book entitled "The Excitement of Teaching." In that book, he said: "With me, teaching is more than an art or an occupation. It is a passion. I love to teach as a painter loves to paint, as a singer loves to sing, as a poet loves to write. Before I get out of bed in the morning, I think with ardent delight of my first group of students.

"One of the chief reasons for success in life is the ability to maintain a daily interest in one's work, to have a chronic enthusiasm; to regard each day as important." That is one of the chief reasons for success in any undertaking . . .

One summer evening, I studied the sales ability of two star-gazing merchants who had set up telescopes at forty-second Street, opposite the Public Library in New York. One charged 10 cents for a look at the moon. The other, who had a slightly larger telescope, charged a quarter.

The one who charged a quarter a look was getting four times as many customers as the one who charged only $0.10. To be sure, you got a slightly better view with the $0.25 telescope dash but the main reason for the success of this higher priced telescope was the personality of the merchant in charge of it. That person radiated enthusiasm and talked about looking at the moon with such excitement, that one would, if necessary, have passed up dinner in order to see it. The one with the 10 cent telescope said nothing and merely took orders. This experience was to me an outstanding example of the value of enthusiasm.

When Sir Edward Victor Appleton, who had been awarded the Nobel Prize in physics, was made chancellor of the University of Edinburgh, *Time* magazine sent him a cable asking him if he had any recipe for success. "Yes," he replied, "enthusiasm. I rate that even ahead of professional skill."

Enthusiasm Rates First

I don't know of anything in the world that will do more for you than enthusiasm. Thomas A. Edison said: "when a [person] dies, if they can pass enthusiasm along to their children, they have left them an estate of incalculable value." Experience proves to be that true. It is more than wealth, for enthusiasm will produce wealth. Not only wealth but great zest for living.

Ralph Waldo Emerson, who is considered the greatest of American philosophers, saw the value of enthusiasm. In one of his essays he wrote: "Every great and commanding moment in the annals of the world is the triumph of some enthusiasm."

Two people in an office have exactly the same kind of jobs. One works in a half-hearted way, as if bored by it and glad to have the hands of the clock point to five. The other works with gusto, finds it exciting, finds each day and adventure. Now which do you think is going to do better work? Which one is going to get ahead?

. . . But enthusiasm is more than just zest for work. It is for the whole of life and living. If you have it, you have a priceless possession. Cherish it.

∾   ∾   ∾

In the next chapter, we'll explore how to not only tolerate differences, but to value them.

Key Takeaways

- The four quadrants of the Johari window are Open, Hidden, Blindspots, Unknown
- It's important to be aware of our blindspots and use self examination to identify the unknown.
- One of the best ways to discover our blind spots is to solicit feedback from others.
- We're not going to love everyone, and not everyone's going to love us. But we can all appreciate each other and respect our dignity
- Relationship Mapping helps us to look at the nature of the relationships we have in our lives and the roles we have in them.
- When creating our relationship map, here are some roles to consider:
  - Personal relationships
  - Suppliers
  - Professional Associates
  - Who I report to
  - Who reports to me
  - Community
  - Peers
  - Customers/clients
- The Little Realized Secret of Success: Enthusiasm

"How do you need to change in order for things to change?"
—Nigel Alston

3: VALUING DIFFERENCES

"Benji, come back here and finish your dinner."

Ernie was at a nice Italian restaurant with his sister and her husband and he was shocked at how she was letting her son run all over the place. When they were kids, their parents would have absolutely never let them leave the table at dinner—let alone run around a restaurant. But then, Ernie's sister also used cuss words around Benji, didn't enforce a regular bedtime, and tolerated a lot more "talking back," than Ernie did with his kids.

Frankly, it bothered Ernie a lot more than he let on to his sister. He wished he could be more tolerant of it and maybe even understand her reasoning. But every time he thought about bringing it up, he backed off. He didn't want to start a conflict with his only sibling.

The Emperor's New Clothes

There's an old parable by Hans Christian Andersen about an emperor who was so fond of new clothes that he spent all of his money buying them. One day, two weavers came to town and, after hearing how much money the emperor spent on new garments, devised a plan. They would convince him that they had special thread that was invisible to anyone who was stupid or unfit for office. The emperor was excited to have such a suit, and paid them a handsome sum to weave it for him. Day after day they sat at their looms, pretending to weave, and finally presented him with a pretend outfit, supposedly made out of the invisible thread. The emperor put the suit on, and was rather surprised that he couldn't see anything. Not wanting to appear stupid or unfit for office, he put it on and went for a stroll downtown. "What do you think of my new suit?" he said. The townspeople were shocked to see him naked, but didn't want to challenge the emperor, so they played along. "It's lovely!" "It flatters you so well," they said. The emperor was proud of the loyalty of his townspeople. Then, a young child broke free from his parents and ran up to the emperor. "You haven't got anything on!" he exclaimed. Soon, the townspeople began to whisper among themselves, "He hasn't got anything on!" But no one dared tell the emperor, and he kept walking, more proud than ever.

This parable highlights the danger we face when we surround ourselves with people who are afraid to tell us the hard truth, to challenge us, or to express differences of opinion. Whether in world politics or in a small friend group, it's important to do more than "tolerate" differences.

We must actively seek them out. Reaching out to others who are different from ourselves is what drives innovation, change, new ideas and thinking, better results, and opens possibilities. As the old saying goes, "If nothing changes, nothing changes." If we stay stuck in our own frames and mindsets, we can never grow. Instead, adopting an open-minded attitude toward people who are different from us can lead to incredibly meaningful connections that would otherwise never happen.

Creative Abrasion

Linda Hill, the Wallace Brett Donham Professor of Business Administration at Harvard Business School, and her co-authors, in their research studying innovation at companies like Pixar, Google, and many others around the globe, found that "Innovation usually emerges when diverse people collaborate to generate a wide-ranging portfolio of ideas, which they then refine and even evolve into new ideas through give-and-take and often-heated debates. Thus collaboration should involve passionate disagreement. Yet the friction of clashing ideas may be hard to bear . . . Often organizations try to discourage or minimize differences, but that only stifles the free flow of ideas and rich discussion that innovation needs."*

This concept is called "Creative Abrasion." In the words of Jerry Hirschberg, founder of Nissan's US automobile design arm, and author of *The Creative Priority*, "Creative

---

* Hill, L.A. et al. (2014) "Collective Genius." Harvard Business Review, June, 2014. https://hbr.org/2014/06/collective-genius)

abrasion recognizes the positive dimensions of friction, the requisite role it plays in making things go. Without it, engines would not work, a crucial source of heat and electricity would be eliminated and relative motion across the surface of the planet would all but cease."

Abrasion is easy. But how do we bring *creative abrasion* into our connections in order to mutually benefit?

It's Easier Said Than Done

Oftentimes, being "open-minded to differences" can be easier said than done. This is especially true when those differences relate to core values that we hold dearly. And, as we saw in the last chapter, sometimes we can have blind spots and not even know we have certain values until they are brought to our awareness. How many times did you not realize you had an opinion about something until you saw a news story or something on social media and had a strong reaction to it? "That's just wrong!" you might have exclaimed, getting angry. "Something like that should never happen." You may not have been aware that you cared about it until you encountered that story or post.

The first step in connecting with those who have different values from ours is to become aware of the values we hold.

Values Awareness Quiz

Following is a self-assessment that we give in our training programs that allows participants to get clarity on how the values they grew up with may still be influencing them today.

Values Awareness Quiz

1. As a child, I was raised to celebrate specific holidays related to my country of origin or religious beliefs.
2. As an adult, I am proud of the culture in which I grew up and the clear rules of behavior I learned.
3. My religion requires me to observe specific traditions as an act of faith.
4. By choice, there are additional observances each year that are important to me based upon my interests, gender, age, or other factors.
5. Most of my associates know little or nothing about my background and values.
6. I believe that religious and cultural observances should be a private matter.
7. I am familiar with the cultural backgrounds and religious beliefs of my co-workers.
8. I respect and celebrate the cultural observances and traditions of those on my team.
9. I openly share the significance of my own cultural celebrations.
10. Only the official holidays of this country should be honored at work.
11. I find some of the customs, traditions, and/or observances of my colleagues to be curious or offensive.
12. Our workplace would be more harmonious if all of us shared the same values.

Values Awareness Indicators

IF YOU RESPONDED "YES" TO ITEMS 1-4

This may indicate a strong connection to your own cultural and religious traditions and values. This may provide you with a strong sense of purpose, offer guidance for ethical behavior, and be a comfort in unfamiliar or stressful situations.

Conversely, your personal experiences and strong beliefs may make it harder for you to appreciate views that differ from the ones you hold.

IF YOU RESPONDED "YES" TO ITEMS 5-6

This may indicate that you are more reserved about openly expressing your own values and believe that others should behave likewise. This approach may avoid conflict and confrontation when differences do exist but, a lack of awareness could actually cause problems based upon insensitive comments or behaviors to which others may take exception.

IF YOU RESPONDED "YES" TO ITEMS 7-9

This may be interpreted as demonstrating openness to others and viewing differences as being interesting rather than irritating. A benefit of these attitudes is that it can lead to building rapport with colleagues.

IF YOU RESPONDED "YES" TO ITEMS 10-12

This may be viewed as being a purist in terms of cultural values and mores. Advantages of this perspective may include fostering a homogeneous workplace when willingly embraced by all. A possible disadvantage is that it can easily alienate members of the group who hold differences of opinions and practice other styles.

As you look at your scoring in the Values Awareness Quiz, were you surprised? Do you agree or disagree with the results? One idea might be to run your results by someone you trust to give you an honest opinion (unlike the naked emperor!) and see if you have any blind spots in your awareness.

Values Exercise

Another way to determine your values is to consider some of the widely held ones and see if you share them. Here is a list of some of the commonly held values. Review the list and circle the ten that are most important (feel free to add to the list!)

Acceptance	Balance	Chastity	Creativity
Discipline	Faith	Grace	Humor
Love	Optimism	Resilience	Self-Control
Tradition	Agility	Boldness	Cheerfulness
Decisiveness	Empathy	Family	Health
Independence	Loyalty	Passion	Resolve
Serenity	Trustworthiness	Ambition	Calmness
Compassion	Dependability	Enthusiasm	Fidelity
Happiness	Integrity	Modesty	Persistence
Respect	Teamwork	Vision	Assertiveness
Candor	Conformity	Devoutness	Fairness
Generosity	Honesty	Kindness	Obedience
Power	Reverence	Thrift	Wisdom

Once you've got your top ten, eliminate half of them to boil it down to the top five things that you value. Then start to notice how the important moments in your life (e.g. the things that cause you great joy or tears of joy) reflect when these values are being expressed. While watching a Ninja Warrior (obstacle course) competition in which his daughter was competing, Michael watched an eleven year old girl struggle mightily to unsuccessfully conquer one of the obstacles on the course. "For two and a half minutes, she clung to a bar, supporting her weight with her arms and shoulders and tried to get the bar to move to where she needed to go. She tried everything, and did not quit! It wasn't until the timer ran out that she finally let go and fell to the mat. She was devastated, and I later honestly told her that it was the best performance of the event because she did not quit! She tried everything she could, but did not give up, even though several other girls abandoned this difficult challenge to run the rest of the course." This gritty performance aligns with his values of persistence and creativity, and for him it was wonderful to see these values expressed so completely.

Similarly, think back to when you've been totally irate at someone's actions, and notice how it probably reflects a violation of one of your top five values. Cam Robertson remembers a time when he was very young and someone who was like a father to him, someone he respects tremendously, used a derogatory term for an ethnic group. Cam, without thinking, angrily snapped "that is not an appropriate term!" Upon reflection, he realized this was a violation of the value of "respect" that is one of his core values. "If it hadn't been such a violation of a core value, I would have been more respectful in how I responded to this gentleman. But it was a visceral reaction that just escaped from my mouth."

The Value of Values

Why should we care about values anyway? Aren't they just internal frameworks for understanding life? The value of values is in how they guide our behavior. Take the value of generosity, for example. Author Daniel Russell talks about how differently "generosity" can look in different circumstances.*

"Sometimes helping means giving a little, sometimes it means giving a lot; sometimes it means giving money, sometimes it means giving time, or just a sympathetic ear; sometimes it means offering advice, sometimes it means minding one's own business; and which of these it might mean in this case will depend on such different things as my relationship with my friend, what I am actually able to offer, why and how often my friend has problems of this kind, and so on."

So, while we may believe we hold certain values, how we express those values is highly contingent on the context. More importantly, our values are important to us! Usually we can't identify where they came from, but they govern our behaviors and interactions with others. And just as

---

* Russell D C (2015) Aristotle on cultivating virtue. In: Snow, N (ed) Cultivating virtue: perspectives from philosophy, theology, and psychology. Oxford University Press, Oxford, p 37–38

our values are important for us, the actions of another are important to them. Which means we have two choices. We can either deem them "wrong!" Or we can respect the fact that their values are real for them and seek to understand (if not necessarily buy-in) how they show up for them.

Types of Values

Values can be categorized in several ways. The ones we're familiar with include:
- Personal
- Religious
- Social
- Familial
- Organizational

When we look at that list, we can see that those are actually contexts within which we express values. Something that is accepted in a family (e.g. devoutness) may not be accepted in a workplace, for example.

A less obvious way to look at values is in terms of how we express them. They include:
1. Things we have (e.g. a fancy watch, the car we drive, art or decor)
2. Things we do (e.g. our work or hobbies)
3. Who we are (how we operate under pressure)
4. Whom we admire and respect (e.g. our heroes or mentors)
5. Whom we trust (e.g. those in our inner circle)

While those at the top of the list are easier to see, it's the ones at the bottom of the list that more accurately reflect on who the person really is.

We can tell a lot about someone (and others can tell a lot about us) by looking at those things. If there's an inconsistency between what one says and what one does, it can be challenging to connect with that person. Emerson once wrote, "What you are . . . thunders so that I cannot hear what you say to the contrary." In other words, your actions speak louder than words.

Using the Johari Window, we can also understand that there are some differences that are visible (such as age, skin color, identified gender, height and weight, et cetera) and other differences that are invisible. These are commonly value differences, such as religion, country of origin, political affiliation, sexual orientation, and other identity-related differences.

R.E.S.P.E.C.T. Find Out What It Means To Me

How can we bridge the gap when we have different core values from another? The graphic on the next page illustrates the method by which we can make the most of our differences.

In the example with Ernie, he had a different set of values when it came to rearing children than his sister did. When he finally approached her in conversation about it, he was surprised to learn that they were not as far apart in terms of values as he thought. By seeking to understand her

RESPECT: Make the Most of Differences

R	Relate to commonalities
E	Explore differences
S	Seek to understand
P	Promote inclusion
E	Embrace new thinking
C	Celebrate uniqueness
T	Tap into possibilities

role as a single parent who had to "choose your battles" in raising Benji, he was better able to embrace a new way of looking at the things he'd been judging.

Master trainer Tom Mangan has some good advice on how to respect someone else's differences.

"Prior to being with Dale Carnegie, I was in the United States Marine Corps for twenty-two and a half years. When I tell people that, they are surprised that I could make such a turnaround. Well, no matter where you go, when you think about it, people are dealing with the same issues, the same challenges. We might wear different clothing. And we might use different terminology, but essentially we're doing the same thing. It's important to understand that aspect of dealing with people. We want to make it as easy as people want to connect with us. How? It has to do with conversations being horizontal rather than vertical."

We'll get more into the nature of conversations in a later chapter, but Tom's point is a good one. Regardless of background, experience, or personality—everyone is dealing with basically the same issues and challenges. We can use the tools taught to us by Dale Carnegie to bridge any apparent differences and get to commonality. Certainly it's not always easy, but when we work to respect and value differences (rather than judge them as wrong), we create the opportunity for "creative abrasion" which can build connection, innovation, new possibilities, and better results.

Take the First Step

Our challenge is to bridge the gap between "knowing" that differences are valuable to "doing" something about it. So think about someone in your neighborhood, in your workplace, your club or your house of worship who is different than you. Next time you see them, rather than retreating to the safety of your usual friends and engage them in a conversation to understand who they are and what's important to them. We'll talk about how to do that in chapter five.

In this chapter, we talked about how it's important to reach out and actually seek interactions with people who have different values than we do. Doing so opens us up to new ways of thinking and connection. Even if we don't agree with what the other person says or does, it's important to be open-minded to the value that embracing differences can bring.

In the next chapter we'll talk about how what we believe shapes what we see, and learn that seeing isn't necessarily believing, and that sometimes believing is seeing.

Key Takeaways

- Reaching out to those different from us drives innovation, newness, better results, opens possibilities, etc.
- Open-mindedness is critical in creating connections
- Creative abrasion is a key driver of innovation.
- Types of values:
    —Personal, religious, social, family, organizational
    —Have, Do, Am, Admire, Respect, Trust
- Types of differences
    —Visible differences "What people see"
    —Invisible differences "Who people are"
- The RESPECT acronym helps us include people who are not like us. It stands for Relate to commonalities, Explore differences, Seek to understand, Promote inclusion, Embrace new thinking, Celebrate uniqueness, Tap into possibilities.

4: FRAMES, FILTERS AND HOW THEY GET IN THE WAY

Ernie was having a bad day. He'd lost a sale that he thought was a sure thing, and he'd been beating himself up about it all day. All of the reasons why he might have blown the deal kept running through his mind. "I'm a terrible salesperson." "It's because I'm not in the same industry as the customer." "They'll never want to buy from me in the future because I didn't make the sale today." "The competitor's product is just better."

As he pulled into the driveway of his home, Ernie's mood was going from bad to worse. "Is there another way I can be looking at this?" he wondered.

Who amongst us hasn't lost a deal, been rejected for a job or a date, or otherwise didn't get something that we really wanted? It's human nature to personalize

it. But, as we've learned so far in this book, many of
the things that we think are about us simply aren't.
When we're trying to connect with another person (or
situation) and get rejected, the concept of frames and
filters can help us gain understanding.

Frames

The idea of frames has been around for a very long time. In 1955, researcher Gregory Bateson said that statements "don't have intrinsic meanings, but only acquire those in a frame that is constituted by context and style."

In other words, if one makes the statement, "The Los Angeles Rams won the Superbowl," the statement doesn't have any meaning at all until the person listening has a frame for it. Where is Los Angeles? What is a "Ram" if it's not an animal? What is a "Superbowl?" What does "winning" mean?

If one has no context for American football, these are just words and the statement has no meaning. If, on the other hand, an American child sees her mother rooting for her favorite American football team, she develops a frame for what football means. If she then grows up and meets someone from another culture who was raised to know "soccer" as "football," a very confusing conversation is likely to ensue.

In other words, our "frame" is a broad understanding of a topic or a situation. It's much like a camera lens that captures certain things and leaves other things out. We can only hear or receive things that come through our frame, and our frames are influenced by our gender, education, relationship with other people, assumptions, personal agenda, sense of efficacy, and more. The experiences we have in the world, the things we learn and observe, all lead to frames.

But the thing is, our frame of a situation is very often unconscious, meaning that we aren't always aware of how our experiences are shaping our perceptions. When Aubrey Percy was a child, she declared The Wonderland Motel in Ithaca, NY, as the best lodging in the world! Now that she's grown and has a son of her own, she realizes it was awesome because it had a heated pool. There was not much else there that we would consider, "awesome." Her son would not be excited at the prospect of staying at this inexpensive and basic motor hotel because "when we travel, we are fortunate to stay in nicer hotels because I have lots of hotel points that I accrue from business travel." Aubrey's son's frame of reference is 3–4 star hotels, whereas when she was her son's age, her frame of reference was 1–2 star motels because her parents were on a tight budget and didn't have hotel points to use.

The Influence of Frames

Our experiences influence how we interpret events. A flash of light streaks across the sky, and people's frames determine what they believe is the cause. Some people think it's a UFO and the government is covering up evidence. Others believe that it is a sign from God that the apocalypse is near. Still others see it as a scientific event, where a gaseous meteor entered the atmosphere. In each case, the person's frame is influencing what they believe and how they interpret the event.

If it's a holiday with a tradition of fireworks, does that change the explanation of the streak of light?

How often have you had it happen where you hear something and automatically assume that it means one thing, and then you get some information that totally shifts your frame? One example might be that you get a voicemail from your boss that says, "Call me as soon as you can." Depending on your frame, you might assume you're in trouble and are about to get fired. But, then you remember that you just landed a major account that brought the company in a lot of money. That might shift your frame to assume that your boss wants to give you a raise or a bonus.

Harold was in an all-staff meeting where the CEO was discussing the company's financial performance for the year. At the end of the meeting, the CEO asked for questions. There were none. So she called on Harold and said, "you must have a question." Harold asked why the goals were such that the company missed them. The CEO said, "great question, I asked the same thing of the executive team," and then gave her best explanation. On the way out of the meeting, several of Harold's colleagues thanked him for asking the question. Feeling pretty good, Harold was sitting in his office when his boss walked in, closed the door and forcefully told him to "never ask questions like that again! It embarrasses the higher ups and angers her handlers." Harold later apologized to the CEO who seemed confused, said there was nothing to apologize for, and thanked him again for the question.

Clearly there were different frames at work here. The CEO wanted a serious question to engage the employees. Harold was curious about what happened with the goals. Harold's boss was either embarrassed or trying to keep Harold from getting in trouble. His colleagues appreciated Harold's courage. Which frame was correct? Hint: if it's your frame, it's correct.

Here's an exercise we shared in the first book in this series, *LISTEN!* What is the first interpretation that comes to mind when you hear the following things?

"Have you eaten yet?"
"Oh, I'm sorry you didn't like the movie."
"Where would you like to go to dinner?"

Here are some different frames for how those statements can be interpreted.

"Have you eaten yet?"

This question could be taken as an invitation to share a meal ("Then, come on over for dinner!"), as a criticism for one's eating habits ("It's 3:00 pm!"), or a factual inquiry of the person's food consumption.

"Oh, I'm sorry you didn't like the movie."

This statement could be taken as an apology for choosing a movie the person didn't like ("I never should have made you watch a romantic comedy."), a hostile comment on the person's taste in movies ("You never like the same movies I like."), or a neutral acknowledgment that the other person didn't like the movie.

"Where would you like to go to dinner?"

This question is a classic argument-starter in many relationships. The question can be received as "Tell me where you want to go to dinner and we'll go there." Or, it can be framed as a set-up for potential conflict, if the receiver answers the question and then the sender doesn't like the choice the receiver makes. "How about we go to Ned's?" "We went to Ned's yesterday." Or it can be framed as the beginning of a dialogue.

It's easy to see from these three examples how a person's frame influences how they hear—and respond to—another person's words. It's also easy to see how the different variables—gender, education, your relationship and history with the other person, et cetera, play into these kinds of situations.

If you have a conflict-filled relationship with your mother, and she asks, "Have you eaten yet?" You are more likely to see that as a critical statement. If your romantic partner says, "Have you eaten yet?" You're more likely to see the question as an invitation to share a meal. Same words, totally different interpretation.

If you have repeated experiences with someone, it tends to create a frame through which you then see ALL of your interactions with that person. And the thing is, we might not even know we're doing it!

Filters

The good news in all of this is that we aren't doomed to blindly follow our often unconscious frames and repeatedly act on the information they give us. We have a choice, and that choice comes from our filters.

While a frame is a "big picture" view of a situation, a filter is a conscious choice to focus more on one thing than another. Using our photography example, the frame is what the camera lens can see. The filter is what it chooses to focus on—what areas are sharp and what are blurry, what areas are light and which are darkened? Cam Robertson showed his wife a stunning photo of a beach in Phuket by noting, "wow! This is stunning!" His wife Susan noticed the attractive and scantily clad woman in a bikini in the lower corner of the photo, didn't notice the scenery, assumed Cam was looking at the nearly nude woman, and Cam got in trouble.

Our filters are the way we can change how we receive what someone is saying. It's important to note that a filter is not a good thing or a bad thing. It's simply a way of managing all of the data that come into our minds. There are so many millions of pieces of data coming at us constantly, that in order to not be overwhelmed, our brain chooses what is most important in the moment.

Choosing to identify our own filters and those of others requires that we maintain a certain level of control over our emotions when we are listening to the other person. It's easy to listen to someone who has the same frame and is using the same filters as you are. It becomes increasingly difficult when you're conversing with someone who sees the world completely different from you.

Johari and Me

The Johari Window model can help us understand that there are some frames we can see that others can too, others that we can see but keep private, others that are our blind spots, and others that are completely unknown. Things get even more complicated when we consider that other people have their own filters and frames about us.

Grace Dagres tells a story about how a woman reframed her experience.

"This woman in our training had been a stay at home mom for twenty years. She got some funding to re-educate herself and to get a job and a career and took one of our Effective Communications and Human Relations programs. She said to me, 'I don't really have anything to share in the class, Grace, because I've just been a mom for twenty years.' Everyone else in the program was from different work backgrounds and jobs. I told her, 'You know what? You probably have the most incredible stories of resilience and empathy, because you've been a single mom for twenty years trying to make the world a better place for your three kids.' She got tears in her eyes and said, 'I've never had anyone say that to me. No one has ever recognized my efforts as a mom as being one of a leader because I've had to lead myself every day.' She came in terrified to take the program, but was able to reframe it that she did have something valuable to contribute. It reframed her entire history."

Why Ernie Lost The Sale—Assumptions

How can Ernie, in our example above, look at his frame for having lost the sale? It's important to consciously look at the frame you have for sales rejection and what filter you use when you receive it. Then you can change the filter to one that allows you to experience rejection differently.

We can use the concept of assumptions to change our frame. For example, what are some of the assumptions people make regarding rejection? What is the opposite assumption? Under what conditions would the opposite assumption be true?

1. I lost the sale because I'm a poor salesperson.

Opposite: I lost the sale not because I'm a poor salesperson. Under what conditions would that be true? "Maybe it's not that I'm a poor salesperson, but that the customer didn't need my product at this time."

2. They bought from the competitor because their product is superior.

Opposite: They did not buy from the competitor because their product is superior.

Under what conditions would that be true? "Maybe it's not that the competitor has a superior product, but that it met one of the customer's other needs. What could that be?"

3. Once I've lost the sale, the customer will always reject me.
Opposite: Once I've lost the sale, the customer will not always reject me.

Under what conditions would that be true? "Maybe the customer will eventually realize that our product really will help them. What can I do to keep the door open?"

By identifying the assumptions you make about rejection (in this case, sales rejection, but the idea can apply to any kind of rejection), you can shift your filter from "I can't handle rejection" to "It's not personal, so I don't mind it."

Bob Eckert and Debbie Allen were teaching the concept of reframing how we see events when a woman in the class slapped her hand on the table, stood up and loudly proclaimed in a surprised way, "I just realized that my divorce wasn't entirely that son of a ——'s fault!" This may well be a great example of Dale Carnegie's 17th principle, "Try honestly to see things from the other person's point of view." For the woman in class, that may have been difficult, but it provided a breakthrough in how she saw herself and the situation.

Frames and Friends

How, then, can we use the Dale Carnegie principles to peel back the layers of frames and filters and create the opportunity to collaborate with those who are different from us? The answers lie in building upon the first set of principles where we work to become a friendlier person and then work to gain cooperation to:

Create a positive environment using these principles:

10. The only way to get the best of an argument is to avoid it.
11. Show respect for the other person's opinions. Never say, "you're wrong."
12. If you are wrong, admit it quickly and emphatically.

Engage the other person in a genuine spirit of cooperation using these principles:

13. Begin in friendly way.
14. Get the other person saying "yes, yes" immediately.
15. Let the other person do a great deal of the talking.

Build understanding of the other person's perspective using these principles:

16. Let the other person feel the idea is his or hers.
17. Try honestly to see things from the other person's point of view.
18. Be sympathetic with the other person's ideas and desires.

Empower the other person by using these principles:

19. Appeal to nobler motive
20. Dramatize Your Ideas
21. Throw down a challenge

The first six principles make it possible to have a conversation where we can engage them to ask genuinely curious questions and be open-minded so that you can determine the other person's frame. Step into that frame, using the filter of being honest and sympathetic to their point of view, even if it's not in your same value system. Be friendly and open and have respect for others, because they, like you, developed their frames from their own life experiences. Your job is not to evaluate whether they are right or wrong, good or bad. Your job here is to genuinely seek to understand their filter, which will allow you to better connect with them.

Kelly, a long-time mountain biker and someone who worked on maintaining her local trails had disdain for the new battery-powered eBikes that were starting to show up regularly on the trails. She disliked how she worked hard to attain the summit of steep and rutted trails while those less committed could cruise up the slope with much less effort. It wasn't until one of her friends offered to let her try one that she realized the appeal. She took it for a quick spin and came back grinning.

"What do you think?" said her friend.

"Wow, that's amazing," Kelly said.

"So you want to get one, right?" her friend concluded.

"Well, they're quick and fun," Kelly acknowledged. "But I enjoy the physical challenge of gutting it out to the top of the mountain. That's why I ride. I'm not going to get one, but I can understand why people like them!"

Now that we've completed Part One of Connect!, In part two, let's look beyond our own Awareness and Mindset and focus on our relationships with others.

Key Takeaways

- A frame is a broad understanding of a subject. Our frames are influenced by our experiences, and this process is often unconscious.
- A filter is a conscious choice to focus more on one thing than another. Our filters are the way we can change how we receive what someone is saying.
- How people view us: what we do, how we look, what we say, how we say it are all influenced by our frames and filters
- One way to change our frames and filters is to consciously identify our assumptions and then reverse them. "Under what condition would this be true?"
- We can use the Dale Carnegie principles to peel back the layers of frames and filters and create the opportunity to collaborate with those who are different from us.
- To connect with others who have a different frame, step into their world and be open-minded.

"If, as a result of reading this book, you get only one thing: an increased tendency to always think in terms of the other person's point of view and see things from that person's angle, as well as your own. If that's all you get from this book, it may easily prove to be one of the stepping stones of your career."
—REBECCA COLLIER

Part Two

Competency and Creating Connection

Action seems to follow feelings but in reality we have more control over action.

In order to connect with others, we have to know what to do. After all, connection is not an individual sport. It just doesn't happen when we are sitting alone. How can we learn how to initiate and cultivate relationships? What role does trust have in connection, and how can we restore it if it's broken? Does conflict have to be the end of a connection? What's the difference between empathetic listening and just "listening?" And, how can we create meaningful relationships when we are virtual from others? Part Two of *Connect!* gives us the answers to these, and many more questions, as well as suggestions and tips for building connections that add value to our lives.

5: INITIATING AND CULTIVATING RELATIONSHIPS

Ernie was nervous. A friend he hadn't seen in ten years called and wanted him to join a group of people at the Getty Museum in Los Angeles. Although they'd been friends for a dozen or so years, Ernie hadn't seen Neil in a long time—not since they were roommates in college. But, Ernie had also promised himself that this was the year he was going to reach out to others and make new friends. What better way than to reconnect with someone he knew before? Despite his openness at the time, when it came to the night before, all Ernie wanted to do was to cancel and stay in his comfort zone.

Relationships Take Work

Whether we are seeking to make new friends, expand our network of work contacts, or connect with customers, initiating and cultivating relationships doesn't just happen. It takes conscious effort. We can't just go down to "Friends R Us" and buy a new friend. And even when we have a circle of connections, we have to make a concerted effort to keep those relationships going. Jeff Shimer explains it this way.

"It's so easy to let our relationships just go by the wayside because you move away. You know, you don't see each other that frequently, whatever connected you at the time is no longer appropriate. It takes effort to keep those relationships going, but it can pay off in spades.

"In 1984 I had six guys in my wedding party that were all very important to me. One was my best friend in high school. Another one was one of my other really good friends in high school. And then others were people I met through college years, a college roommate, a guy I knew through scouting, but, and I'm happy to say that I'm still close friends with a good number of those people. We stay connected through social media and that's been a real great thing to be able to stay connected with them and feel more involved in their lives and vice versa. But it's still that phone call that, Hey, let's get together. And so last summer, I'm celebrating my sixtieth birthday and I decided to take my kids and a few other people for a weekend trip to New Orleans. I posted it on my high school Facebook page and figured I'll get a few people who might want to come. Well, my one good friend from Dallas who was at my wedding, he's one of those close high school friends said, 'Hey, we'll be there.' And so he and his wife came over and, well, I don't know what we were thinking, but it was the weekend that a hurricane came through.

We ended up getting stranded—fourteen of us! My two twenty-two year old daughters thought it was great fun, and I ended up blowing a bazillion hotel points on a suite downtown, where we got stuck there for four days with no power or air conditioning. We had a deck of cards and some supplies. Eventually, though, we needed to get out. But, there was no gas and no rental cars. There's just no way out of town. So my friends from Dallas had come for my party and just stayed the one night and then immediately left the next morning. They called me and said, "You need to get out of town. I have a vacation home in Destin Florida you can use. This guy packs up a big SUV with emergency supplies and drives from Dallas to New Orleans to get us (this is not a short drive—like an eight hour drive). He takes time off work to drive and get us and take us to Florida (another four hours). He helped us get a rental car and put us up at his own home in Florida. It was amazing. A lifelong relationship with a friend who's willing to not only come celebrate with you, but also rescue you when it's needed."

Part of connecting is determining and really setting an intent and a vision that this is going to be a long-term relationship, and then flexing with what you need to do to make that work.

Conversation Starters

So, how can you go from meeting a total stranger to creating the kind of friend who'll come rescue you in a hurricane? It all starts with a conversation.

Many people don't really know how to actually start a conversation. We're not taught! We just meet someone and start talking about ourselves or ask about the weather. One technique we teach is called Conversation Linking. The idea of it is that we link topics together in our minds.

Conversation Starter "links"

- Nameplate
- Home
- Family sitting down to dinner
- Work glove
- Air travel
- Tennis racket
- Lightbulbs

Visualize that you're walking up to the front door of a house. On the front door is a large brass, engraved nameplate. Can you picture it? The front door is attached to a lovely house. It's the house of your dreams, right down to the color, the windows and the style. Can you visualize the house? As you look inside the front window, you see a family very similar to yours sitting down to eat your favorite meal at the table. Make sure you can see the family in your mind. As you look at the front door, on the door handle, you see a work glove. It's a brown leather work glove that looks really well made. Yes, a work glove on the door handle. Just sitting there on the handle. Make an image in your mind of it.

Now as you glance up, you see a brightly colored airplane flying overhead. You can just see inside and you can tell that people are smiling and enjoying the flight. It looks like fun, yes? Oddly, out of the pilot's window, you can see that the pilot is holding a tennis racket. Yes, a tennis racket out the window! It's an unusual sight, but it makes you smile. Especially when you notice that with the tennis racket, the pilot is swatting at lightbulbs that are popping into the sky. Light Bulbs! What a sight! Have you ever seen anything like that before?

Hopefully you just saw all that in your mind.

Now read the two paragraphs above again, and create a vivid image of the—admittedly odd—scene in your mind. Make sure you can vividly see it so that you can remember it.

We've given you an image that you want to remember because it links to the list above that represents key topics of conversation useful so that you can engage and connect with someone new by starting a mutually interesting conversation.

The technique of linking is based on the idea that our mind remembers through pictures and the more exaggerated the picture the more we remember it. When we link pictures together, it helps us to remember even unrelated items. The best questions allow for a long answer, and being a good listener is critical to building and strengthening relationships. Here are some examples.

The name plate represents:
- What is your name? Is it short for something? Have you always been called that?
- Tell me about the background of your name?
- How do you spell that?
- Are you named after anyone? What do you know about them?

The House links to these conversation starters:
- Where do you live?
- What brought you to your current location?
- How long have you lived there? What changes have you noticed?
- What do you like about living there?
- Where did you live before? What do you miss about it?

The Family sitting down to a meal links to these questions:
- Tell me about your family.
- What activities or traditions do you enjoy doing as a family? What do you enjoy about them? How does it keep you connected?
- (Note: You will want to avoid asking any questions that could be considered uncomfortable. For example, "Are you married?" or "Do you have any children?")

The brown leather work glove represents these questions:
- Where do you work?
- Tell me about your work?
- What do you like best/least about your job?
- How did you get started there?
- What got you interested in your profession?
- If you weren't at this organization, what would you be doing? (Work is the most comfortable area for many of us to discuss.)

The brightly colored airplane links to these questions:
- Do you enjoy travel? Tell me about your favorite place you've been to so far?

- Do you travel with work? Have you been anywhere you never thought you'd visit?
- Where would you like to travel? What's your dream destination?
- Where have you gone on vacation?
- What are you planning to do for the next holiday?

The tennis racket that the pilot is holding out the window refers to these questions:

- What hobbies do you have? What do you like about them? Why are they interesting to you?
- What activities are you involved in/do you watch when you are not working? What do you enjoy about them?
- What do you like to do for fun? Tell me about it?
- How did you get involved with this hobby?

The Light Bulbs popping out of the air represent ideas, which you can cover with these questions:

- Ask some questions based on current events (local, regional, national, or international).
- Ask some questions about ideas based on the event that's happening around you (e.g. a networking event, a social event, a work event).

If anyone needed this approach early in his career, it was Jonathan Vehar. When applying for his second job, his potential new boss, Lisa Hamilton, took him to lunch. The interview went well, and Lisa was interested in his job-related skills, but she told the recruiter, "he didn't say anything during lunch!" What she meant was that he didn't ask any questions and behaved as the introvert he is. Yes, he replied to her conversations, but he says, "I didn't know what to talk about. I'd asked all my questions about the job, the people and the company and I didn't know what else to say!" For his follow-up interview, he had a number of questions prepared (at the strong urging of the recruiter), and got the job. But he almost lost it by now knowing how to start a conversation. The conversation links would have saved that lunch and built a solid connection much faster.

Getting Horizontal

Tom Mangan gives an interesting take on the Conversation link. He suggests that to form deeper connections, we resist the urge to go vertical.

"So one of the things with the conversation starter links is that there's an implied directive to go vertical to get higher and higher to the next question . . . Instead, how can you keep it horizontal? In other words, if I ask you about your name or if I ask you your name, a lot of us are like, okay, I know your name and boom, run on to the next thing already. Better yet, explore it some more. 'Tell me about your name. Why do you have an interesting spelling with your name? Why is it spelled that way? Did you change it or did your parents name you that?' Then, last names can be another whole topic. We can have a 20 minute dialogue on just your name. That's what I mean about going horizontal. Don't just jump up to the next topic, but stay with one for a while and dig deeper.

"And then the same thing with the next one up; the house that they would picture. 'And so tell me, not just about where you live, but what do you like about it?' Or 'What keeps you there?' More and more are working remotely. So what's keeping you living in this town when now you really could live anywhere in the world? This is what gets us remembered and what lets us remember others. It allows you to go deeper in your connection. It's not like I'm just checking things off a list."

In other words, rather than going from the nameplate to the light bulb in rapid succession in as few questions as possible, take time to explore each topic in depth before moving to the next image. This creates even more commonalities that form the foundation of a connection. "Oh you also have a twelve year old daughter?" or "My family is also from Italy!" or "I just discovered how much fun pickleball is." When you find these common interests, you can find even more commonality that serves to connect the two of you.

How to Remember Names

Have you ever had it happen that you asked someone their name and then promptly forgot it one minute later? It can be embarrassing at best and a connection ending faux pas at worst. We have come up with a myriad of ways to handle forgetting someone's name, from simply calling them "Sir" or "Ma'am"or "Dude" or "Buddy" to getting someone else to elicit their name. What if, instead, we focused on actually remembering their name in the first place?

Dale Carnegie knew that a person's name is to them "the sweetest sound," and created an acronym to help us remember names. It's called the LIRA formula.

1. Look and Listen
Try as hard as you can to focus on the person speaking, and make sure you understand very clearly what their name is. You might ask them to spell it.

2. Impression
Create an impression in your head of what the person looks like. This includes physical features or the surroundings / situation in the moment.

3. Repetition
Repeat the person's name as many times as possible in conversation. Use it when it is appropriate. Use it when you are saying goodbye to that person. Afterward, repeat it in your head as much as possible.

4. Association
Make associations of physical characteristics, names of landmarks, objects, buildings, companies, etc. Use color nouns and similar words to help you remember the name. We as humans remember things better in pictures.

After using this, remembering names becomes that much easier. Use names with everyone you interact with, practice this and make it a habit.

Frank Starkey shares how remembering names actually landed him some business.

> Years ago I was asked to go in and speak to a leadership team at a company. Well, they wanted to know a little bit more about Dale Carnegie Training. And so someone said, "Hey, I need you to go in and, and talk to 'em for an hour or so about what Carnegie does and how we can help them and all that kind of good stuff." So I went to their offices, but then I had to wait and wait past my appointment time. So my hour turned into maybe thirty minutes. I walked in and instead of me being in a room full of people, we were all seated around this conference table, which is the worst kind of way to make a connection, because everybody was just seated around and they have their laptops and their tablets all sitting in front of them. They did a quick round of introductions and then we talked about Dale Carnegie Training a little bit and then talked about their company. There were eleven people from the company all seated around the table. And at the end I thanked them each by their first and last name. They were so amazed that I knew their first and last names! They were impressed and felt important that I would remember each one by name. They later told me that this is how we got the business.

Names matter! If we walk into a room of strangers convinced that we're not good at remembering names, that we'll immediately forget them, or that we can't get everyone's names, we'll be right.

A young candidate for state senate met Blair Miller at a fund-raiser in a friend's home. A few years later, Blair was at a fund-raiser for this same candidate when he ran for US senate. The candidate remembered Blair by name, and asked about his three kids, whom he remembered from the previous conversation, despite the fact that the politician met hundreds of strangers every week! He remembered because he was interested, he paid attention, and he cared. Whatever happened to that young candidate? He eventually became a two-term president of the United States. His name is Barack Obama.

Instead of thinking we can't remember names, let's be intentional about remembering the name of each person we meet. When we ask for their name, or when they tell us their name, stop. Let it sink in. Ask some questions. Use the LIRA technique described above, rather than just plowing into the next question. Dale Carnegie's sixth principle says, *"Remember that a person's name is to that person the sweetest and most important sound in any language."* If we want to make a connection or a new buddy, call them by their first name. Don't call them "buddy." Especially if you're running for office.

The Art of Telling Stories

Although a lot of what we're sharing here talks about eliciting information from others, a conversation is always a two-way experience. It's not a conversation when we pepper people with questions or respond with one word answers. Imagine during the conversation that there is a spotlight shining on the person doing the talking. We absolutely want to be interested in them and do a great deal of the talking. But at times the other person will turn the spotlight onto us, and we need to share who we are as well.

In that case, we may need to tell stories or engage the other person with our own ideas. How can we do that without "hijacking" the conversation and making it about ourselves? Here's something we shared in one of the other books in the series, *Speak!* on how to tell a good story.

To tell an authentic story, we need to remember the three E's: 1) you must have **Earned the right** through experience of study to be able to talk about your subject and tell your stories, 2) you must be **Excited** to share, without trepidation or hesitation with enthusiasm, and 3) you must be **Eager** to share because you want to convey value to the listener.

It all comes back to being yourself. Assuming the three E's are there for you, then trust that you are interesting enough in your own right.

When the spotlight is on you, it's because the other person is interested in you. But that's not enough for you to just tell your story. Your goal should be to make a connection to the conversation or the question in order to share the spotlight and put it back on them. If the person asks you about your hobbies, and you tell her about how you love to run marathons, you might then make the link to her love of playing guitar. "I imagine that as much as I run several days a week, you probably practice your guitar a lot too?" or Reply in kind, "Do you follow any sports?" or

"What do you enjoy doing outside?" or "I enjoy running with other people. Do you play guitar in a band?" or "I prefer to run outside rather than on the treadmill. Have you ever performed in public? What was that like for you?"

There are those people who will take the opportunity of a question to hijack the conversation until it's time to go home. Let's not be one of those people. Let's not avoid the spotlight, but let's also be sure to take turns enjoying the spotlight and enjoying listening to the other person.

The Innerview

Another technique we teach in our course that allows people to make even deeper connections is called The Innerview. This is not a typo. We're not talking about an "interview." Conducting an "Innerview" is a proven method of deepening our connection with our people through an intentional conversation that seeks to uncover what's inside a person, rather than just focusing on what's on the surface (remember in chapter 3 when we talked about digging deeper beyond what people have? This is how to do that). While the Conversation Starter Links are about starting a conversation, the Innerview seeks to dig deeper to understand someone at the level of values and beliefs.

In the Innerview process, we converse in a way that generates information and connection. This isn't designed to evaluate or judge someone, like a traditional interview, but instead simply ask questions for the purpose of understanding commonalities from which we can build our connection.

Three Types of Innerview Questions
1. Factual questions

These are questions that are typically conversational in nature and revolve around factual information. The answers to these questions are occasionally found in personnel files. Examples of factual questions are:

- Where did you grow up?
- What kind of activities were you involved in as a kid?
- Tell me about your first job.
- What were your interests in school?
- Tell me about your family.
- What do you do for fun?

2. Causative questions

These are questions to determine the motives or causative factors behind some of the answers to the causative questions. They are typically "why" and "what" questions. Examples of causative questions are:

- Why did you pick that particular school?
- What caused you to study that ?
- What brought you to your current job?
- What direction did you go in right after high school?
- How did you get involved in that hobby?

3. Values-based questions

These are questions to help connect with a person's values system. They are designed to help a leader hear what a person feels is important. They are also questions that people rarely ask, but give a greater view of the inner person. Examples of values-based questions are:

- Tell me about a person who had a major impact on your life.
- If you had to do it all over again what, if anything, would you do differently?
- If there were a major turning point in your life what might that be?
- There are many highs and lows as you go through life. Are there any of either that had a significant influence on you?
- What words of wisdom would you give a young person if he/she sought your advice?
- How would you sum up your personal philosophy in a sentence or two?

As Tom Mangan told us earlier when talking about "going horizontal," the goal of the Innerview is not to get through all of the questions as quickly as you can, nor is it even to cover all of the questions. The goal is to understand the other person, find commonalities and get to know them as people, not just their job title, role, or responsibilities. As we have said, connecting is about relationships. The Innerview helps build that in both directions.

Connections Can Surprise Us

Rebecca Collier shares a story that illustrates that you never know where a connection with someone might lead.

> John was a relatively new business development director for a California-based accounting firm and he had a target list of contacts that he wanted to make. One

of those contacts was the CEO of a major healthcare system. Following the first session of a Dale Carnegie course, John and I talked about how specifically this could be used in a networking environment. John went to an event with the hopes of being able to meet the CEO. And he was just surrounded by people. So John struck up a conversation with a woman who was kind of off on the fringes of the group and he was practicing this conversation technique and they had an absolutely brilliant time just back and forth. She, according to him, was fascinating and he learned so much about her. And as they were finishing up their conversation, lo and behold, who walks up to the two of them but the CEO? The woman turns to him and says, John, I'd like you to meet my husband. To the husband she says, "You need to talk to this man."

Connections sometimes happen like that. And we need to be open to them even when it's not necessarily part of our "strategy." You never know who can help you out, and having connections with other can enable that. A platform like LinkedIn is useful to see if we know connections to people with whom we want to speak. Being open to conversations on the bus or subway or airplane can be like that as well. Aubrey tells of a dinner with some friends of her husband, Rodney, that Aubrey was meeting for the first time. These friends became very close and they enjoyed many dinners and social gatherings together. When she asked "how did you and my husband meet?" Aubrey almost spit out her drink when the reply was, "on the subway." Similarly, Rodney has also created friendships with both an advertising legend and the father of a very famous rock star. He met them when out walking their dog.

More than twenty years ago Blair Miller was sitting on an airplane headed home when he struck up a conversation with the woman sitting next to him. Turns out she was a musician and was going to be performing in his hometown. They had such a great conversation that she offered him tickets to the show and asked him to come backstage and introduce her to his wife (about whom Blair had been effusing) after the concert. This woman turned out to be Diana Krall, the famous musician . . . before she was famous. Needless to say, it was a great show.

We are seeing time and time again that by having an open attitude and a natural curiosity about others, we can make genuine connections. You'll notice that John didn't scan the room for whom he thought could connect him with the CEO. He struck up a conversation with someone who was just standing off to the side. He could have waited until it was his turn, or elbowed his way in to speak with the CEO, but he took the opportunity to make the connection. And that made all the difference.

Advice from Grandma

Grace Dagres shares more about connecting with people for who they are and not what they might do for us.

> Too often, we don't necessarily take the time to connect with people for who they are as a person. We

don't get to know their traits and characteristics and their incredible stories. Instead, we focus on their title or their position. "How long have you been a VP?" for example. But my grandmother told me that even the King of Greece puts on his pants the same way as everyone else. What she meant was that no matter your status, whether you're a CEO or the person who cleans the building, someone we meet in an elevator or someone we meet in a boardroom, we have to treat them the exact same way because we are all just people.

People think those that are famous or important are different. They may be famous or "important," but they're still people. Dave Huntley was waiting with a video crew for the CEO of a large company to arrive so they could record an interview with him. While they were waiting, the crew was playing billiards at a pool table on set. When the CEO walked in, everyone froze. Dave asked, "hey Tom, do you want to shoot some pool?" The CEO stopped and thought about it. Then said, "as much as I'd like to, I've kept everyone waiting long enough. So let's do this." The offer to shoot pool was an invitation to a connection that the CEO turned into an opportunity to acknowledge the people in the room and the fact that their time was important. This formed the foundation for the connection necessary for people to feel comfortable enough to create the environment for an authentic interview.

Remembering this can really help when we're feeling social anxiety about meeting new people. Everyone—even people with different backgrounds, religions, politics, titles or other differences—has something in common with you. It's just a matter of finding it. That's the basis of connection.

Communication Style Differences

Madison was excited and nervous. She was three months pregnant and it was time to tell her employer so they could prepare for her impending maternity leave. She needed signatures from people—her direct supervisor and the woman in Human Resources. They each had very different communication styles, and it was important to handle this correctly.

First, she went to her boss, Bill, Bill was a very direct communicator who was very analytical and commanding. If she went in there and told him the whole story about how she and her husband had been trying to conceive for years and were about to start IVF treatment when they got pregnant on their own, she'd lose his interest after about five seconds. It wasn't that he was a jerk who didn't like her. He was just that in terms of communication.

"Hey Bill. Do you have a minute?"

"Sure, Madison, come on in. What can I do for you?"

"Well, I have some good news. Steven and I are pregnant!"

"That IS great news!," Bill said, smiling and nodding at his family photo. "Joan and I have three boys. Is that your maternity leave form for me to sign? When will you be starting your leave?"

Madison handed him the form. "July first."

Bill scribbled his signature and handed back the form. "Here you go. Congratulations again, Madison. You're going to be a wonderful mother."

Shutting his office door, Madison smiled. That went perfectly! But she knew that things would be a little different when she went in to tell Cheryl from HR. Cheryl was an indirect communicator who was very friendly and demonstrative. If she went in there with just the facts, Cheryl's feelings might be hurt. It was going to take a lot longer to get the signature.

"Hey, Cheryl, can I come in?"

"Sure, Madison. Sit down! How have you been? I don't think I've seen you since you got food poisoning at the company picnic three months ago." Cheryl smiled and waved Madison over to the couch, where she joined her.

"Yeah, about that . . . It wasn't food poisoning after all. Turns out, I'm pregnant."

"Girl, that's GREAT. I know you and Steven were trying. Have you told your parents yet?"

Twenty minutes later, Madison left the office with both of the signatures she needed. By understanding Communication Style Differences and adapting hers to the style of the other person, she was able to deepen her connections with both Bill and Cheryl.

Communication Styles

Research on communication styles will commonly place people into one of four categories:

FRIENDLY. Casual, amiable, relationship-focused, helpful, warm, from the heart; likes positive feedback.

ANALYTICAL. Formal, methodical, systematic, logical, data-oriented; seeks answers, details, and solutions; likes evidence.

DEMONSTRATIVE. Demonstrative, expressive, uses gestures, paints the big picture, and likes to hear what's in it for them.

COMMANDING. Efficient, focuses on goals and objectives, strong viewpoints and opinions, decisive, likes to be presented with options.

Adapting Our Communication Style

It is important for us to adapt to the person or people we are speaking with to put them at ease. Here are some suggestions on how to do that.

- Establish rapport based on the style in which the other person communicates
- Spend time on what is comfortable for the individual
- Use pacing and appropriate language that suits the other person's style
- Be conscious of time based on the other person's style
- For groups, adopt a friendly style

This is one of those situations where the golden rule—"treat others as you'd like them to treat you"—doesn't work. You'll want to apply the platinum rule: "treat others they way they'd like to be treated." Otherwise you risk doing what's right for you, but wrong—and ineffective—for them.

Six Levels of Positive Feedback
or Empty Praise vs Solid Praise

Another element to initiating and cultivating relationships is giving praise and feedback. How we do this can nurture our connections or weaken them.

Imagine your boss or a loved one walks up to you and says, "I need to give you some feedback." How does that make you feel? Most times, we take a deep breath and prepare for the worst. Yet feedback shouldn't be only about things we're doing wrong. It should also be positive to let us know what we're doing right, so that we will know that we should keep doing it. In fact experts and research tells us that the ratio of praise to criticism should be at least five to one if we want to change behavior. At least. People who are working under the constant barrage of negative criticism become demoralized and disengaged.

Lee was leading a complicated online training program that involved two technology platforms, a co-trainer, and a producer. The participants were located on the other side of the world, which meant Lee was working very late at night. The co-trainer wanted Lee to train it the same way that Pat, the other trainer, delivered the program. Lee, who was very experienced, had other ways of delivering the content with different analogies, demonstrations, and stories. But that's not what the co-trainer wanted. Every time Lee did something slightly differently—even when not knowing how Pat did it—Lee was criticized. "That's not the right way to do it." "What are you doing?" "That was a mess." Lee noticed that rather than being excited about delivering the program and what they could bring to the course, that they were feeling cautious, shy, unwilling to display humility and ask questions about the "right" way to do it, and stopped offering suggestions or contributions that would have made the program better. Lee noticed that they felt like they were in a toxic workplace and that it was shifting their behavior.

When employees are feeling criticized, they begin to cover up mistakes and hide issues that need work. That's not productive! We want to engage them. We want to build them up. We want to give them positive feedback. A praise to criticism ratio of at least five to one helps make that happen.

When expressing positive feedback:
- Be sincere, not manipulative
- Be specific to provide meaning
- Be brief for the sake of clarity
- Be quiet when you're finished to allow the recipient to accept it

As we mentioned in another book in this series, *Lead!*, there are six levels of positive feedback, which we sometimes call praise. Praise is a "polite expression of admiration." Positive feedback lets someone know what they are doing right—those things we want to ensure that they keep doing—even as they change other behaviors. Praise and feedback help your followers grow and flourish, as long as they perceive it as being sincere and specific to them.

The six levels range from giving feedback about things that are impersonal to those that are very personal.

6. Level of Vision: This is the highest form of compliment, as it is the most global. "You really get the concept of customer service."

5. Level of Identity: These are things that are core to a person. "You are an important member of the engineering team."

4. Level of Belief: These are more internal qualities about the person. "You have a positive outlook."

3. Level of Skills: "You're great with Photoshop."

2. Level of Behavior: Things that are observable. "You did not interrupt when Janet was telling you about the problems with the project."

1. Level of Environment: Things like your car, clothing, home, or office. "I like the new artwork on the wall."

When you are giving feedback, strive to bring up your feedback to a higher level, because the lower levels have less impact than the higher ones. Would you rather be complimented on the color of your shirt or receive positive feedback which acknowledges how well you deliver on the vision. The higher the level of feedback, the more someone feels understood and acknowledged based on who they are, rather than things that are easily visible.

Here are some examples of how it works.

Instead of "Your PowerPoint was very thorough" (environment), try "I really appreciate how you ask other team members questions to engage them in the project" (behavior).

Or "You're really good at organizing things" (skills), becomes "You are a really organized person (identity)." Or even, "You helped all of us be more organized (vision)."

Notice how much more effective the feedback becomes when it is backed up with something you noticed.

Compare:
"You're really responsible"

to
"I like how you remembered to be on time to our meeting even though you were working through that customer issue" (behavior). "You're really responsible" (Identity).

Compare:
"You're a great listener."

to
"You're a great listener (skill). It's a pleasure to have someone of your caliber in our organization" (identity).

Why? A person's identity can only be formed with the proof of what you actually noticed. They will really believe you think he is a responsible person because you pointed out an example of when he was responsible.

Think about how you feel when you get an "empty compliment" such as "You're one great guy!"

As opposed to a "solid compliment" such as "Wow you remembered my work anniversary. You're one thoughtful guy!"

Strength Words

Using variety in the kinds of strength responses that we make promotes integrity, adds credibility, and moves us closer to the target of raising awareness on hidden strengths. For example, below are forty different strengths that we could observe in others.

Assertive	Spontaneous	Direct
Subtle	Progressive	Perceptive
Versatile	Profound	Partnering
Impartial	Judicious	Trail-blazing
Orderly	Diplomatic	Imaginative
Modest	Systematic	Open-minded
Unstoppable	Collaborative	Natural
Energetic	Wise	Assured
Insightful	Supportive	Enterprising
Illustrative	Constructive	Composed
Innovative	Balanced	Empathetic
Eager	Inquisitive	Honest
Alert	Receptive	Charitable
Commanding	Rousing	Leadership
Genuine	Resilient	

Beware of empty praise/feedback!

Remember earlier when we talked about the *laissez faire* boss who let people do what they want and gave praise that had no substance? That doesn't count in our five to one praise to criticism ratio goal. We should not tell an employee, "You're the best!" without any specific feedback because it has no meaning. Nor does it reinforce specific behaviors we want to continue to encourage. The best at what? What should they keep doing? Although it is a start and may be better than giving no positive feedback at all, the goal is to be as specific, effective, and believable as possible.

Another trap is telling an employee who is really not helpful that he is wonderful. People can tell how we really feel about them, and if we give false praise it leads to dissonance. "I'm getting terrible performance evaluations, but she's telling me how great I'm doing."

When we can't find anything to praise we need to dig deeper. Even behavior that is expected can be genuinely acknowledged. "I appreciate that you're here every morning ready to work the phones." "I like that you are working to learn our complex product lineup so that you can represent the company better each day."

How to Give Feedback That Isn't Praise

This isn't to suggest that the only kind of feedback we should give is positive. There is an art to giving constructive feedback but it is an important part of the feedback loop. As Dale Carnegie stated, it's best to call attention to the person's mistake indirectly (principle #23) and to start with one of your own (principle #24). Here are some specific guidelines about how to give feedback as a strategy of building connection since when we learn to give effective, behavior-based feedback, we develop more trusting relationships with people while sharpening our own leadership and communication skills.

Behavior-Based Feedback

1. **Begin with praise and evidence**. "I appreciate that you deliberately take the time to coach your team."

2. **Relate the reason to change—why is this feedback important for them?** What's in it for them to hear and adjust to the feedback? "Would you like to be even more effective at coaching people? This could improve the relationships and engagement of the team. This could help everyone be more successful which would reflect well on you, their leader."

3. **Be behavior-specific and focus on things that can be changed**. "You're too tall" isn't helpful. Identify the specific behaviors that could be improved. "When you stand over people and look down on them when you're coaching them, people feel ill at ease."

4. **Be concise** (be careful not to overwhelm the person). Don't get into the story of the development of coaching, the research that you've read about it, or give thirty-seven examples of where you've seen it done right or wrong.

5. **Be encouraging**. Position it as easy to correct or modify. "If you were to sit down with them face-to-face, you can make people feel more comfortable."

By using this concise five-step process, we are able to provide feedback on how to improve. And while it may sometimes feel uncomfortable to receive the feedback (although others crave it!), it demonstrates a level of candor and respect that builds on the foundation of the connection that we have together.

How to Receive Feedback

If we're going to be giving feedback to others, we should invite and welcome feedback from others. And as much as we might hope that they're as good as giving feedback as we'd like to be, that might not be the case. And that doesn't invalidate the value of their feedback. So here are some guidelines for receiving feedback:

- Assume that we are not objective when assessing our own capabilities. That means we need help. There are a variety of 360-degree feedback tools available that can provide insight into the perceptions of those with whom you work.

- Prepare yourself for feedback. It can be difficult to set egos aside, and many people benefit from learning adaptive techniques that help them approach and accept feedback constructively.

- Appreciate the intent. While getting feedback that reveals blind spots can be uncomfortable, remember that it's also difficult to give constructive feedback. Chances are, those providing it are trying to help.

- Disrupt routines. We are blind to the things around us when we become set in our own ways and fall into routines regarding how we engage others, including reacting to issues, running meetings or coaching our employees.

- Just do it. Given the importance of these leadership behaviors, there's no downside to simply taking action to become even better at them. The simple act of learning can also encourage greater self-insight, which means there's twofold benefit to taking action: becoming aware of and simultaneously working to improve one's performance of these crucial behaviors for motivating employees.

- Say "Thank you." Feedback is a gift that takes courage for people to give. It is an investment in their time and effort—and a risk—to offer feedback to you. Even if the feedback stings, appreciate the other person for the feedback that they offer. Don't just mumble, "thanks." Instead, look them in the eye, and let them know how this feedback is helpful to you. Be grateful for the gift.

We can never completely eliminate our blind spots; they are part of human nature. But through candid self-reflection combined with focused effort, we can safely steer ourselves toward becoming the exceptional people that we want to be. Better yet, you can ask others for feedback which demonstrates respect for the other person, shows that you value their input, and continues to build connections.

With self-awareness, adopt what is known as a "learner's mind." Be open and curious, be okay with making mistakes and being wrong. Even if we strive to have impeccably high standards, we must leave our ego at the door.

In this chapter we've explored how to initiate relationships and how to flex our communication styles around the other person's, as well as how to give and receive praise and feedback.

Key Takeaways

- Relationships take work! We have to invest time and emotional energy into maintaining our connections.
- We aren't taught how to make conversations. Conversation Links can help.
- Horizontal conversation links mean to stay in one topic and go deep.
- A helpful acronym for remembering names is LIRA: Look and Listen, Impression, Repetition, Association
- When telling a story, remember the three Es. You have to have Earned the right, be Excited, and Eager
- When giving an Innerview, there are three types of questions: Factual, Causative, and Values-Based
- There are four different communication styles (Friendly, analytical, demonstrable, commanding) and it's important that we adapt to the style of the other
- There are six levels of feedback:
    6. Vision
    5. Identity
    4. Belief
    3. Skills
    2. Behavior
    1. Environment

- Give positive and negative feedback in a ratio of five positives for every one negative piece of feedback
- When expressing positive feedback
    —Be sincere not manipulative
    —Be specific, it provides meaning
    —Be brief for clarity
    —Be quiet, which allows the recipient to accept it
- When expressing negative feedback
    —Begin with praise and evidence
    —Relate the reason to change
    —Be behavior-specific and focus on things that can be changed
    —Be concise
    —Be encouraging
- When receiving feedback:
    —Say "Thank you"

"Everybody knows somebody who knows somebody who knows somebody."
—JEFF SHIMER

6. BUILDING AND RESTORING TRUST

Ernie's neck was getting stiff from craning his head backwards trying to get the waiter's attention. He'd asked for a glass of water three times, and still hadn't gotten it yet.

"I'm starving. I hope they bring our appetizers soon." Ernie's sister looked at her watch as she said this. "I have to get home to relieve the babysitter soon."

It was their parents' wedding anniversary, and Ernie and his sister decided to go to the Italian restaurant where their dad proposed to their mom. Throughout their lives, the family had celebrated special events here, and Ernie even knew the owners personally. But, in the last couple of years, since the pandemic, the quality of the food and the service had changed. The last time Ernie and his sister came, it took three hours for them to get through dinner.

> *At the time, Ernie was inclined to be sympathetic because many restaurants had been struggling at the time. But, eventually the smaller portions, the lack of customer service, and the higher prices were starting to take a toll on Ernie's trust in the family-favorite restaurant.*

In the Dale Carnegie white paper, "Trust is Dead. Long Live Trust! Why Long-Term Customer Loyalty is Still Driven by Trusted Relationships," we shared the results of a large study we conducted looking at the relationship between trust and loyalty. We looked at the things that lead up to a trusting relationship and things that come out of one. In the case of that study, we were looking at an economic relationship (salespeople and buyers), but the issue of trust is obviously important in any kind of relationship. You can't have a meaningful connection with someone you can trust but who doesn't trust you. And certainly not with someone you don't trust.

What Is Trust?

When you ask people "What is trust?" The answer most people can agree with is that "you know it when you feel it." Our research showed that there are two parts in the definition of trust: 1) credibility and 2) concern for the other person.

Trust is an essential ingredient in the initiation and maintenance of connections. If a person orders food from a restaurant to be delivered, and time and time again the order is wrong or the customer service is bad, trust will erode. On the other hand, if most of the time the order is correct, and when there is a problem, customer service is there to help, the restaurant will have credibility and demonstrates concern for the person.

The more important the connection, the more important trust is. We'll allow more mistakes in a restaurant order than we will with our bank. If they make one mistake with our money, that's a red flag. If there's a second? We're looking for another bank.

So some level of trust is required to establish a positive relationship and, as that relationship grows over time, it provides opportunities to reinforce trust; they become interdependent. This means that the trust has to start somewhere. What we say is, "once they've earned the trust, I'll trust them." The reality is that if we start with trust, that will accelerate the cycle of reinforcement. Which means that if our default is trust, that will increasingly foster trust in the relationship.

Beyond trust, relationships also require a commitment on the part of both parties and a willingness to make short-term sacrifices to maintain the relationship. Investing in the relationship and creating confidence in its stability are actions that further develop positive relationships. In turn, positive relationships create personal commitment since the more trusting a relationship becomes over time, the higher the value a person places on the relationship. The outcome is that the person is likely to be more loyal to the one that they trust rather than risk uncertainty with someone they don't know.

Trust + Relationships = Loyalty

Laura Nortz shares an example of a relationship that she has that has developed into a powerful sense of trust.

> There's a gentleman that I used to work with, a leader who had developed a strong connection with me. We had a high level of trust—to the point that if he ever said, "Laura, we need X, Y, Z done and here's why," I'd do it. Why? Because I knew he had my best interest in mind. He would never ask me to do something that was self-serving. This isn't to say he wasn't going to benefit from whatever he was asking me to do. But, I knew that it would be something that would benefit me too.

Remember, trust is about credibility and, as illustrated in Laura's story, concern for the other person. Laura knows that the leader has her best interests at heart.

As we've mentioned several times in this book, developing meaningful connections with others involves an intent from the start to create long-term relationships rather than transactional ones. Or, if the nature of the relationship is transactional (our Postmates example, as one) that it still goes deeper to make a genuine connection.

How to Build Trust, Credibility, and Respect?

How do we go about developing trust, credibility, and respect? These three outcomes are critical for building connection. The following graphic illustrates the criteria on which we are judged. Right or wrong, like it or not, this is how people see us, and it determines whether or not we'll be trusted, have credibility, or be respected.

1. How we look	+	2. How we act	+	3. What we say	+	4. How we say it	=	Trust Credibility Respect

Taken together, these four criteria form either a favorable or unfavorable impression, and they all factor into the connection and the extent to which we or others feel a sense of belonging.

1. **How we look**: would you immediately trust a brain surgeon if she looked like a heavily tattooed biker? Would you make a donation to someone raising money for poor children if they parked a new Rolls Royce in your driveway?

2. **How we act**: If someone talks about how important honesty is to them, and then you hear them misleading co-workers about the status of a project they're leading, could this cause mistrust?

3. **What we say**: If someone made an inappropriate joke at our expense in a meeting, what happens to the level of trust? Or if they tell you that they didn't pay someone for work done on their behalf, would you trust them?

4. **How we say it**: If we mumble, it's nice to meet you while looking at someone else, how does that land? Or if someone tells us everything is going great, but they look frazzled, stressed, agitated, and like they haven't slept in days, are we likely to believe them?

We cannot build connections with people if the four criteria above aren't appropriate to the situation. If we're at a Harley Davidson gathering, tattooed bikers would look like they belong, and someone in surgical scrubs would look out of place. If we're paying extra money to get a project done as quickly as possible, then someone looking frazzled, stressed and sleepless might make us feel like they're doing everything possible to complete the project. There are no right answers to these items other than being authentic to who you are and appropriate for the situation.

Jayne Leedham shares a story about the importance of trust in her as well as her work and how what she says and does and how she says it can lead to dramatic transformation.

My job is to turn up to a business or a company and go into a room with twelve to twenty people who have been told they're going to a training course. They don't necessarily want to be there, and in some cases are rather hostile about it. So my job is to really quickly connect with those people, reassure them, and to earn trust in them so that they will follow through the process of what I'm going to do next. Most importantly, I value their day. So a big, big part of that to me is to openly say, "You've given up so much time for this and your time is so valuable. It is highly appreciated. I'm gonna make it worth your while."

I think when I first started out, I didn't get that enough and I didn't make enough connections. So some people at the end of a day would still feel like a hostage in the room because I didn't see that it was my job to make them see 1) the value of the course and feel 2) that I'm going to give them something worthwhile, make their life easier in some way.

These days by the time I've been in a room with them for an hour, I will know every single person's name. My aim is to also know their job—and not just the job title but what they actually do.

Once I understand that, I can start sharing examples or asking questions that are really relevant to their world. And that's where they feel that we're more connected and that what I'm doing is all about helping them. As a Dale Carnegie person I really do use the first nine principles to build that trust with every participant in the room. And because of that, I get great results. And it's the first thing I tell new trainers: "Now don't worry about the content in front of you. Because if you can't connect with them, you can't do your job. You can't get in the door, their mind. This is especially true when they are being asked to deliver training. So for you to be able to like everybody, have a good laugh about it and let's just learn some stuff. It makes the connection that much better."

David Kabakoff agrees. Yes, the content is important, but, "It's not about the content but how it changes you. The essence [of building relationships] is to put the other person first. If you don't, there is no chance to build trust. One time, in the classroom, there were two very different participants. One was a younger black man and the other was an older white man. It didn't seem like they were going to have much to connect on, but we used the linking technique to help them find out about each other. After all, if I find out about you, then we can trust.

It turns out, both of the men had been abandoned as babies. It morphed into a conversation that built a tremendous connection—all because the trust that was built created a safe environment for them to be genuine and honest.

> *"Creating the environment of trust*
> *is the precursor to connection."*
> —DAVID KABAKOFF

Twenty principles for Building Trust, Credibility, and Respect

1. Build rapport by taking others' interests to heart. Ask questions, learn what motivates them, and create an environment for growth and learning.
2. Listen sincerely—with your ears, eyes, and heart— while being aware of prejudices and judgment.
3. Honor and find merit in differences of opinion, biases, and diversity.
4. Ask, don't tell. Collaborate with others in decisions, display an open and accepting attitude, and be receptive and open-minded to new ideas and constructive feedback.
5. Be willing to negotiate and compromise, and be a mediator among others who have different points of view.

6. Think before speaking. Consider the audience, relationship, and environment when choosing your words and actions.

7. Think and speak in terms of "us." Use inclusive language and appropriate emotions. Communicate with diplomacy, tact, and sensitivity.

8. Take care of issues promptly. Speak confidently, decisively, and with authority; offer evidence when stating opinions. Use instincts and facts to make sound and rational decisions.

9. Demonstrate integrity. Stand up for your beliefs and important non-negotiable values.

10. Remain humble. Be visible and show your team that you are "in the trenches" with them. Be a modest expert and be willing to defer to others' expertise.

11. Adhere to high standards of professional and ethical behavior. Be honest and reliable, keep confidences, fulfill promises, and keep commitments.

12. Be patient and dependable and act consistently, rationally, and fairly. Be resilient and bounce back from setbacks quickly.

13. Be a stellar role model—act professionally and always walk the talk. Demonstrate good will and good intentions. Give people the benefit of the doubt, believe in honest mistakes, and let people off the hook when appropriate.

14. Demonstrate respect, trust, and faith in others. Delegate, empower, and let go. Encourage risk-taking and provide support.

15. Be authentic—demonstrate congruency between your words and actions. Reveal your own thoughts and feelings frankly and openly and provide constructive feedback as needed.

16. Be generous, courteous, approachable, and available as a resource. Treat people with compassion and dignity.

17. Be realistic when communicating vision, goals, and outcomes. Offer opportunities for growth, training, and mentoring.

18. Be human. Accept responsibility and admit mistakes, downfalls, and disadvantages.

19. Deal directly with others. Do not partake in gossip, spread rumors, or talk behind someone's back.

20. Be an ally. Focus on strengths, offer encouragement, and build their confidence. Show appreciation, give recognition and give others credit for accomplishments

Can We Be Too Trusting?

Of course, almost everyone has had the experience of placing their trust in the wrong person. Or losing the trust of someone they cared deeply about. Similarly, we've all met people who are inherently distrustful and approach the world as a scary, untrustworthy place.

The key is to have a balance. The following graphic illustrates the "sweet spot of trust." As you read it, assess yourself using the grid below the graphic to understand where you are on the scale, and where you might need to intentionally shift a bit.

Trust Assessment

When we trust ourselves, another person, or an object, we possess an assured reliance on the character, ability, strength, or truth of that person or thing. Too little trust or too much trust can be dangerous. We achieve a healthy degree of trust when we use a balance of facts and instinct to make good decisions and exercise good judgment.

Healthy Trust

Excessive Trust   **Responsible Trust**   Excessive Distrust

Where am I on this scale?

Excessive Trust	Healthy Trust	Excessive Distrust
Trust everyone blindly and recklessly	Trust people based on instinct and information	Trusts no one, including oneself
Can be naïve and gullible	Is discerning and cautious	Can be suspicious and paranoid
Tends to fall for scams and make poor decisions	Tends to be responsible, exercise good judgment, and make good and confident decisions	Tends to be paralyzed by insecurity, protectiveness, and indecision
Often has a passive "yes" attitude	Has an assertive "maybe" or "possibly" attitude	Often has an aggressive "no" attitude

Grace Dagres shares a story about turning around someone who'd begun to fall too far on the "distrust" end of the spectrum.

You have to build trust quickly. You gotta show people your appreciation, you gotta really listen to them to really understand what they're saying to you and make them feel important and be genuine about it. I got a phone call from a friend, around the beginning of 2019, who said to me, "my daughter finished university. And for the last year she has been depressed. She can't get a job. So she stays in her room and she's really sad. And I have to do something to help her because she's remarkable. The world just doesn't know it yet." He asked me to work with his daughter in the Dale Carnegie course on Effective Communications and Human Relations. He believed that it could have a great impact on his daughter, so I agreed. We had a call online and she said, "I don't think you can help me because I'm not really good at speaking up. I'm very introverted and I'm the last person to be assertive. In fact, I don't know how to be direct and how to speak with confidence. I'm terrified."

I knew I needed to gain her trust, so I said, "I believe you. I remember being your age and how scary it was to sell myself so I could get a job. And I'll make sure that I create a safe and comfortable environment for you to take a risk and get uncomfortable." So she said to me, "okay, I'll do it." Well, you know what? She showed up every week, the first couple of weeks she was pinching her skirt or her pants on the side whenever she had to speak to the group.

One day, in meeting six, she showed up and actually volunteered to go first! I asked her, "What happened between meetings five and six?" She had a job interview! She went to the interview and used the principles of how to build trust and create relationships right away with the interviewer.

And then they told her she got the job on the spot. I asked her, "What do you think made the difference?" She said, "Grace, I really sincerely made it about the other person. Because, what did the interviewer want? They want to be recognized for hiring the right person. So I gave them all the reasons why hiring me would make them look good."

This is a perfect example of someone applying Dale Carnegie's 17th Principle, "Try honestly to see things from the other person's perspective." Not only did Grace's student see it, she then adjusted how she looked, how she acted, what she said, and how she said it to get the job.

Warning Signs of Distrust

How can we tell when someone in a relationship with us is beginning to have distrust? Here are six warning signs of distrust:

1. Low morale, lack of motivation or initiative
2. High absenteeism, lateness, turnover
3. Guarded communication or an active rumor mill

4. Undercurrent of fear or worry
5. Cynical or suspicious behavior
6. Defensive or aggressive behavior or communication

The degree to which trust is an issue may be determined by the symptoms. Here are a few examples:

Occasional trust issues	Serious, ongoing trust issues
• Doing the minimum to get by • Avoiding challenges • Sleep-walking through the day • Lack of commitment	• Acting out: demonstrating negative attitude • Focus only on problems and obstacles • Resist change • Undermine/sabotage others' accomplishments

Where Do Trust Problems Come From?

In Grace's example, she met the girl through a previous relationship that she had with the girl's father. That's not always how we meet people. Sometimes we encounter others whom we have a natural distrust of, or who might distrust us naturally. It might even be apparent before we have a single interaction with the other person. Where does this come from? How can we restore trust when we weren't the ones to create mistrust?

The answers go back to the idea of frames and filters. We all have life experiences that shape how we frame situations, and that can cause an element of distrust. If, for example, a person had a terrible experience in school, with harsh and punitive teachers, a poor education, and maybe even dropped out of school, they are likely to have a natural distrust for the education system in general and teachers specifically. Now imagine that this person is at an event and they find out that the person they're talking to is a school administrator or a teacher. There will be an element of distrust that's already there, even before the people have said hello.

What can be done to restore trust? Shift the filter. The way to do this is to, as we have been recommending throughout the book, make it about the other person. If you're the one who had a tough time in school and you find yourself talking to a teacher, put your own experiences on the back burner and ask engaging questions of the other person. "Why did you get into education?" "What do you like about your job?" "What motivates you to go into the classroom everyday?" If you're a teacher who is talking with someone who doesn't trust educators, ask meaningful questions that allow for a deeper connection. "What did you enjoy about your education?" "Did you ever have a teacher who believed in you?" "What is it about the education system that didn't work for you?" Our guess is that both sets of questions will create some commonalities that form that basis for a connection and perhaps even trust.

Restoring Trust

What if the distrust comes in an already-established relationship? What do you do if trust has been broken? Can it be restored? Yes, if both parties are open to it. The following graphic illustrates the cycle of restoring trust.

In this graphic, 1) represents the event that breaks the trust. That might be a broken promise, or something overheard, or what we hear from others. 2) This causes an emotional reaction to the event which can take many forms. We then 3) disengage from the person/team/entity that broke the trust. To rebuild connection, it's important to acknowledge and 4) discuss what happened with the offending party. Understanding that the event may not have been part of their intention, or that we misunderstood, or that there is an explanation may well give us the opportunity to give them 5) a second chance. When we are intentional about looking for reasons to trust them again, rather than searching for reasons to distrust them, we will find them. This is true for searching for evidence that we shouldn't trust them. When we see 6) that positive outcome, and see them as trustworthy, this 7) restores trust.

Actions to Restore Trust

What are some specific actions we can take to restore trust?

1. Put our ego aside, be humble. We (or the other person) may have a valid reason for the distrust. But holding on to it won't help to restore trust. Recognizing that "to err is human" makes it easier for us to understand the other person, rather than holding them to an impossible standard.

2. Review perceptions. This means looking at our frame to see where our perception might be off.

3. Take a breath or take a break. Having conversations about what happened when we are feeling emotionally charged makes the conversation more difficult.

4. Meet privately. Public accusations rarely make things better or create an environment for humble and honest reflection.

5. Ask for their perspective. This involves getting into their frame and seeing things as they see them.

6. Find out what the other person needs. Sometimes it's an apology, sometimes it's enough to just drop it and move on.

7. Uphold your end of the deal. Clearly, if you agree to do something to restore the trust, you have to uphold your end of the deal!

In this chapter, we talked about one of the core issues in connecting with others—Trust. In the next chapter, we'll get into another core element in relationships—conflict.

Key Takeaways

- Trust involves two things:
    1. Credibility and
    2. Concern for the other person
- Trust requires us to go first
- Trust + Relationships = Loyalty
- Trust, credibility and respect involve four criteria:
    1. How we look
    2. How we act
    3. What we say
    4. How we say it
- It is possible to have excessive trust and excessive distrust. We need to find a level of healthy trust
- There are six warning signs of distrust
    1. Low morale, lack of motivation or initiative
    2. High absenteeism, lateness, turnover
    3. Guarded communication or an active rumor mill
    4. Undercurrent of fear or worry
    5. Cynical or suspicious behavior
    6. Defensive or aggressive behavior or communication
- Trust problems come from our frames and filters

- It is possible to restore trust. Here are seven actions that we can use to do so.
    1. Put our ego aside, be humble
    2. Review perceptions
    3. Take a breath or take a break
    4. Meet privately
    5. Ask for their perspective
    6. Find out what the other person needs
    7. Uphold your end of the deal

7: CONFLICT

Ernie sat in the conference room tapping his foot nervously. The company had hired a new person to head up the marketing department, and historically sales and marketing had a contentious relationship. What's worse is that the new guy had gone to college at Ernie's crosstown rival and then had worked at the biggest competitor in the industry. It was as if conflict between the two men would be inevitable.

The door opened and in walked Bert. Upon initial impression, Bert looked to be as much of a jerk as Ernie had suspected. He had an arrogant swagger and a disdainful smirk. "So, you're the Ernie I've been hearing about," he said as he pulled out the seat at the head of the conference table. "You don't look like I thought you would."

"What does that mean? Ernie thought. "I already don't like this guy."

Not Everyone Sees Eye To Eye

Have you ever met someone and the instant you met them, you knew you weren't going to get along? Frank Starkey has, and he offers some good advice on how to overcome it.

"Did you ever meet someone for the first time and go, We don't see eye to eye. We're not gonna get along. She's from here. I'm from there. We're just never gonna figure out a way to connect. She sees things differently than I do. And then all of a sudden, once you get to know them, then the criticism goes away because you understand where they're coming from. Once you understand and you can figure out how to find the points of agreement, then you can work together.

"Even in healthy organizations, not everybody sees eye to eye with everything. It's okay to be healthy and have disagreements, but you still have a point of agreement. We don't have to agree on everything, but in order to move forward, we have to find a place or a point we can agree on. This is how you get along with people you may not like, personally."

Jonathan Vehar owned a consulting company, and another consulting company started reaching out to some of his contractors to offer them work. This did not sit well with Jonathan. At an industry conference, the CEO of the rival consulting firm approached him, and said, "we should have a conversation." Jonathan, who had been intentionally avoiding the CEO, stiffly replied, "you mean about our contractors?" The rival said, "No. Although we could talk about that. I want to talk about the fact that I think that what we do is complementary, and that we could both help one another." Eventually, the two had dinner and discovered that they were both interested in different parts of the market, and began referring work to each other. In the process, they were able to keep their stable of contractors busy, which created increased loyalty from the contractors. Twenty years later, they are close friends and still working together with their complementary offerings.

What is Conflict?

Whenever you have two or more people, conflict is inevitable. From toddlers fighting over a toy to business owners arguing over contractors to world leaders fighting over country boundaries, conflict is a part of everyone's life.

What exactly is conflict? Here's our working definition. Conflict is . . .

1. A sharp disagreement, as of interests or ideas, emotional disturbance; to be contradictory or in opposition.
2. A mental struggle resulting from incompatible or opposing needs, drivers, wishes or external/internal demands.

As you can see, there are two sides to conflict—external and internal. One is a disagreement with another and the other is inner mental struggle. We talked at length in an earlier chapter about how to overcome inner, mental struggle using the idea of frames and filters. In this chapter, we'll focus more on interpersonal conflict and how to resolve it.

Characteristics of Conflict

Before we can approach conflict with the idea of resolving it, we need to understand the nature of conflict and how people respond to it. Here are some of the characteristics of conflict.

- There is rarely just one source in the conflict.
- Emotions are high.
- People are uncomfortable with conflict.
- People feel alone and that they are the only one going through this.
- People think about what they are going to lose.
- People think that they don't have enough resources to deal with it.
- People can only handle so much conflict.
- People sincerely believe that they are right.

Conflict Originates from PRIDE

Where, exactly, does interpersonal conflict come from? We've devised an acronym that shows the most common areas where people have conflict. It is PRIDE, and the following graphic illustrates it.

Where Does Conflict Originate?

P	Process
R	Roles
I	Interpersonal Issues
D	Direction
E	External Pressures

In essence, we tend to have conflicts with others over Process (how we are doing something), Roles (whose job it is to do something), Interpersonal Issues (you don't have similar styles or have a complicated past), Direction (disagreements over a course of action), or External Pressures (these can be money or resources, other people like children or in-law, time crunches, or anything that is outside the relationship). As we think about the conflicts that we have in our lives, being able to identify the source frequently provides insight and the opportunity to discuss that area with someone else as a way to seek common ground. What is it that we both want?

Six Things That Cause Conflict

Carnegie Master Ercell Charles shares the six reasons why people disagree with each other.

1. They don't hear one another
2. Different values/beliefs
3. Personality styles
4. Different perspectives
5. Generational/cultural differences
6. They just don't like one another

> *"Not everyone is going to like you. You're not a taco."*
> —INTERNET MEME

How to Deal with Conflict

All too often, conflict is hidden. It can be the so-called "elephant in the room." We've all had it happen when we walk into a room and there's tension there for no apparent reason. That's a hidden conflict. However, we can't solve a problem that we don't identify, and so it's important to bring conflict out into the open. But, it must be done strategically so that the conflict doesn't escalate and get worse. Here are some tips on bringing conflict out into the open.

1. Address issue when tempers are cool
2. Choose a neutral setting
3. Treat as a team problem, if appropriate
4. Invite conversation by beginning in a friendly way
5. Use open-ended questions
     —Tell me about why you're angry?
     —What can I do to help you?
     —What caused this to happen?
     —How did you react when we said that?
6. Use "I" or "it" messages rather than "you" messages: "You don't know what is going on around here" versus "I feel like I'm the only one who knows what is going on with this situation" or "It seems that there is a lack of shared awareness about the current situation."
7. Talk about the problem not the person
8. Stop talking and listen
9. Act on what you hear to gain and keep trust

It makes things worse if you listen to someone's feelings about a situation and then disregard what they've said. Remember one of the ways to restore trust that we shared in the previous chapter: Uphold your end of the deal.

Renee and Courtney had a shared deliverable at work related to the rebranding of the electronics company for whom they worked. Renee headed up marketing, and Courtney headed up product management. In order for both of them to be successful in rebranding the products' packaging, Renee had to provide logo and branding guidelines so that Courtney could create all new packaging for hundreds of products. Courtney kept asking Renee to sit down and work on the project. Renee refused to start the project which created pressure on Courtney, knowing that the time she had to do the work was getting critically short. Finally, in a phone call, Renee exploded, "I don't care about what you need!" and hung up the phone. Courtney was stunned. They'd had a good working relationship and socialized outside of work. Courtney decided to let the situation cool. A few days later, Courtney got Renee on the phone and took responsibility for the conflict. "Look, I know that I've been pushing you too hard on this project." Then asked what was really going on. It turns out Renee had been dealing with some health issues and was having trouble with the branding agency who was responsible for the work and was under pressure from her boss. As the conversation unfolded, and as they intentionally worked to understand the other person's point of view, they were able to agree on a path to move forward that would enable both of them to get what they needed.

Conflict Response Scale

Below is a graphic that illustrates various responses to conflict. On the far left are the avoidant behaviors and to the far right are the more aggressive responses. We want to strive to achieve the middle ground, where we are compromising (without compromising what is most important to us) and collaborating so that both sides win.

Conflict Resolution Questions

In order to do this, and achieve a win-win, here are some questions that need to be addressed.

1. What is the conflict?
2. What are the conflict response styles involved?
3. What are the causes? What is the root cause?
4. What are the possible resolutions?
5. What is the best resolution?

Psychological Safety

In order to achieve this, an environment of psychological safety must be present. In February of 2022, a video circulated of a senior Russian military official being interviewed by Russian President Vladimir Putin. In the video, it was clear that the official disagreed with the invasion into Ukraine.

Needless to say, it was not an environment where the official was psychologically (or even perhaps physically) safe to disagree with the President, and so he verbally obliged.

By contrast, in Google's famed "Project Aristotle," they found that one of the hallmarks of high-performing teams was that there was an environment of psychological safety. In this environment, team members feel safe to take risks and be vulnerable in front of each other. In order to truly move past conflict, both parties have to feel psychologically safe.

Psychological Safety

A condition in which human beings feel included, safe to learn, safe to contribute, and safe to challenge the status quo—all without fear of being embarrassed, marginalized, or punished in some way. Timothy R. Clark, 2020

Here are nine signs of low psychological safety:

1. People don't ask many questions during meetings
2. People don't feel comfortable owning up to mistakes or place blame on others when mistakes are made
3. People avoid difficult conversations and hot-button topics
4. Leaders tend to dominate meeting discussions
5. Feedback is not frequently given or requested
6. People don't often venture outside of their job descriptions/roles to support others
7. People don't ask one another for help when they need it
8. There are hardly any disagreements or differing points of view
9. People don't know one another personally. Just professionally or based on the group scope.

The good news is that even if our work, organization, or community social unit is in the early stages of creating psychological safety, we don't need others to start cultivating it for ourselves. When we change our mindset we can empower ourselves to change our behavior and get different results and be a role model for others. This creates yet another basis for connections.

Managing Emotions During Conflict

Conflict researchers Roger Fisher and William Ury, in their classic text *Getting to Yes,* mention several techniques for managing emotions during conflict. Strong emotions are both a cause of, and a result of conflict. People in conflict may have a variety of negative emotions—anger, distrust, disappointment, frustration, confusion, worry, or fear. Here are some tips, based on Fisher and Ury's work, for managing those strong emotions and building an environment of psychological safety:

1. When you feel yourself getting emotional, step back and focus on what the other person's emotions are. Are they angry or just excited and passionate about the subject?

2. Look to find the source of the emotions. What are their filters in the situation that could be causing their feelings and actions? Is it possible that the filter has nothing to do with you?

3. Talk about the other person's feelings openly. "It seems like this conversation is making you frustrated. Am I misreading it?"

4. Express your own feelings in a non-confrontational way (using "I" statements instead of "you" statements.) "I suppose I am feeling disappointed because . . ."

5. Validate the other person's feelings and their right to see something differently than you do. "I can see why you feel that way given your perspective on the situation."

6. If the other person isn't able to step back from their emotions, then you are the one to do it. Don't react emotionally, but step out of the room and give both people a chance to calm down.

When We Disagree

As we've mentioned, it's inevitable to have disagreements. What matters is not that we disagree, but how we handle the disagreement. The way to handle disagreements is to find some form of bridge, using the points of agreement. The following graphic illustrates this process.

Use the Point(s) of Agreement as a Bridge

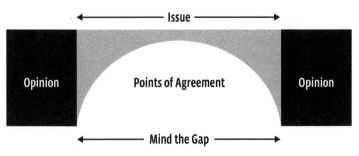

| ← Issue → |
| Opinion | Points of Agreement | Opinion |
| ← Mind the Gap → |

• I hear what you are saying about the importance of . . .
• I see now where you are coming from based on . . .
• _____ can be a very emotional topic.

In order to find points of agreement, there are five steps:

Being willing to find points of agreement that are necessary to bridge the conflict requires us to (once again)
let go of our ego and listen to the other person and their
opinion. Once we've heard it, we ask questions so that we
truly understand the other person. These questions are to
clarify our understanding, not to convince the other person
(Not "Well don't you think that . . ."). As we're listening,
we need to search for the areas where we disagree, which
can be difficult if we're in the mindset of looking for areas
to argue about. Focus on the commonalities. Then articulate them. Where do you agree? Where do you have
common ground? Where do your goals and beliefs align?
Once you're clear where you agree, you have a choice to
reframe the discussion towards areas of agreement, or you
can choose to "agree to disagree," and do so in a courteous
and friendly manner.

Rebecca Collier shares a powerful story about managing conflict. "I was working for an international oil
shipping company—and I mean big oil tankers and huge
containers. One assignment was at a shipping terminal with
the port authorities and longshoreman and it was a rough
and tumble kind of group. In this group were two people who unbeknownst to me at the beginning absolutely
hated each other. Annette and Carl had such an acrimo-

nious relationship that it was affecting other aspects of the operation. After I found this out, I noticed that they sat as far away from each other as possible during that first day of the training."

There are activities throughout the Dale Carnegie course that cause us to engage in conversation and to be paired up with each other, to be in small groups together. And over the course of our five days together, they got to know each other and found out that when they talked about non-business related issues, they really had a lot in common. And what was interesting was in the final session—and it was choose your seating every day—they chose to sit at the same table. When we talked about the benefits that they were taking away from the program, Annette was the first one to stand up and say, "I know I'm not an easy person to get along with. And it's caused me to have a lot of conflicts in my career. And what this program has done for me is it's built a relationship. It opened a door with Carl where we can now have respectful conversations because we know that we have more in common than we do differences." The whole room just stood up and applauded. It was a huge piece of self-awareness for her. For both of them, really. It improved their ability to get things done instead of being at cross-purposes.

Does this mean that all enemies can become besties if we just talk it out? No. But it does mean that we can move beyond conflict and find points of agreement, and that can have powerful benefits and create important connections.

The following graphic shows six options for handling a volatile or challenging situation.

1. **Get cerebral**: in other words, get out of your emotional mindset and think about it using your intellect, rather than your feelings.

2. **Ask for input**: don't try to solve it on your own. Get input from the key stakeholders so that you can get a fresh perspective

3. **Take a hike**: usually you don't need to resolve it right now, and if you're in a volatile situation, you may not be able to. Go for a walk, give yourself some time, and settle down from an excited state

4. **Reflect**: take time to think it through from multiple perspectives and articulate what's working, what's not working, and how you might make it better

5. **Sleep on it**: this phrase is so common because it works. While you're sleeping, your brain will work

on processing it and you may well wake up with fresh insights.

6. **Pick your battles**: we don't need to attend every argument to which we're invited. There may well be value in avoiding the argument. Does it really matter? Is it worth the effort, energy, credibility or collateral damage to fight through it?

Robert walked out of a meeting so irritated that he had to get outside otherwise he was going to quit right there on the spot. Despite his vociferous objections, his team had been tasked with the project that no one wanted because it was almost impossible. Despite wanting to protect his already overloaded team, he was unsuccessful and felt oppressed. As soon as the meeting was over, Robert stormed out of the meeting into the cold Illinois winter and did multiple laps around the warehouse to cool off. As he walked, the neuro-chemistry in his brain changed and helped him move from irate to frustrated to annoyed to nervous to curious about how he was going to accomplish this project that had been dumped in his lap. Towards the end of the walk, he had a realization about how they could accomplish the task in a way that had never been considered before. He rushed back into the office, drafted a plan and started building buy-in from the key stakeholders. This approach led to the trans-formation of the business and created the foundation for the company's digital transformation. All because instead of quitting, he "took a hike."

Dale Carnegie's Tips on How to Move Beyond Conflict

- Try honesty to see things from the other person's point of view.
- Don't fuss about trifles.
- Cooperate with the inevitable.
- Decide just how much anxiety a thing is worth and refuse to give it more.
- When fate hands us lemons, try to make lemonade.
- Never try to get even with our enemies.

This is not a book focused on conflict. It's focused on making connections with other people. And remember we started this chapter by talking about the fact that conflict happens both inside our brains and externally with other people. Certainly when we're in conflict, connections aren't happening. And in fact conflict is like an acid that erodes the connections that we've made with other people. It forms distrust, it breaks down respect, and it can erode our credibility. Rather than discounting or disconnecting because of a conflict, let's take the higher road and build a bridge over the conflict and back into a productive relationship. That's how we grow our connections.

Key Takeaways

- Conflict exists inside ourselves and with others
- Conflict originates from PRIDE: Process, Roles, Interpersonal issues, Direction, External pressures
- Here are six reasons why we disagree:
    1. We don't hear one another
    2. Different values/beliefs
    3. Personality styles
    4. Different perspectives
    5. Generational/cultural differences
    6. We just don't like one another
- Here are nine steps to bring conflict out into the open
    1. Address issue when tempers are cool
    2. Choose a neutral setting
    3. Tread as a team problem, if appropriate
    4. Invite conversation by beginning in a friendly way
    5. Use open-ended questions
    6. Use "I" or "it" messages rather than "you" messages
    7. Talk about the problem, not the person
    8. Stop talking and listen
    9. Act on what you hear to gain and keep trust
- To resolve conflict, we have to actively seek out the areas where we disagree and find areas of commonality, even if it's just that we can "agree to disagree.

• Psychological safety is a condition in which human beings feel included, safe to learn, safe to contribute, and safe to challenge the status quo all without fear of being embarrassed, marginalized, or punished in some way. This is a precursor to conflict resolution.

8: EMPATHETIC LISTENING—Being Humble Enough to Listen

"Ernie, you're not listening to me." Ernie's wife was standing in front of him with her hands on her hips and she was angry.

"Yes, I am. You were telling me about your sister and her first day on the job and how she got lost on the way to the ladies' room and ended up in the men's room instead."

"That's not listening, that's repeating back to me what I just said. You may be hearing me, but I can tell you're listening to the race in the other room."

"No I'm not!" (Yes, he was.)

"Let me ask you. Who is winning the game?"

"Ferrari" Ernie knew he was in trouble with this line of questioning.

"Now, where does my sister work? What's her new job?"

"Uhhh . . ." Ernie knew he was busted. "I'm sorry, honey. You're right. Let me turn off the TV in the next room and I'll listen and pay attention this time."

Is it possible to connect with other people without listening? Have you ever had a conversation with someone about something where you felt so well listened-to that you felt an emotional connection with the other person? For those of us who've had that experience, we know that someone paying attention, listening, and not just hearing us can make a difference. Too often, we listen and our goal is to be able to say something that shows we understand, that we can help the other person by offering breakthrough advice for the other person, or that just allows us to say our piece.

Unfortunately, listening to another person requires the humility to recognize that we won't fully understand the other person until they're done speaking. And nine out of ten our advice is stuff they already know.

Listening Versus Hearing

"But, I'm already a great listener. I can repeat back exactly what someone tells me, word for word!"

There is a huge difference between listening and hearing. Sure, you may be able to hear, and then repeat back the words someone has said. But does that mean you've *listened*? Not necessarily.

Hearing is involuntary. It's when the sound vibrations of vocal expressions hit your eardrums. There probably have been many, many times when you didn't want to be hearing something, but couldn't turn it off.

Listening involves hearing, but also involves understanding. It is a participatory activity, which means you have to engage and participate in order for listening to occur. It requires concentration and awareness so that you can take what you're hearing and give meaning to it.

We've all been in conversations where the person repeated back our exact words, but it was clear they still didn't have a clue about what we were trying to say. In fact, the "repeating back" technique is actually taught as a listening skill, in the form of "Active Listening."

Here's an example. Two friends are sitting around talking about work. One friend works in Information Technology (IT), and the other does not.

The IT friend says, "So, it's so cool at work. We've been working on creating a new SSL VPN solution that will enhance BYOD mobility and offer seamless connectivity while securing our corporate resources. I can't wait until it's ready."

The friend who doesn't work in IT might be able to repeat back what she heard. "SSL" "VPN" "BYOD mobility." But unless she actually understands those terms, she has no idea what her friend is saying or what it means. And, it's not only the technical terminology that matters. How does her friend feel when she is talking about this? What does the information mean to her? Just because someone is speaking and you are hearing their words doesn't mean that you're actually listening and understanding.

Most people would say that they are pretty good listeners. In fact, in 360 degree assessments of managers (where the manager is rated by his or her boss, peers, and direct reports), there tends to be a huge gap between the manager's self-perception as a good listener and what other people have to say. In other words, you may THINK you're an excellent listener. But, are you?

Here's a quiz that we shared in the first book in this series, *Listen!*, that can help you assess your own listening skills.*

Can You Hear Me Now?

For the following questions, answer on the following scale (try to be as honest with yourself as possible).

Not at all   Rarely   Sometimes   Often   Very Often

1. When I'm on the phone with someone, it's fine to respond to emails and text messages at the same time as long as I'm listening.
2. When listening to another person, I start to get upset and react emotionally.
3. I feel uncomfortable with silence during conversations.
4. If I have a relevant story to share, I'll interrupt the other person to tell it and then get back to letting them talk.
5. People seem to get upset during some conversations with me and it seems to come out of nowhere.

---

* https://hbr.org/2008/04/so-you-think-youre-a-good-listener

6. To keep the conversation flowing, I ask questions that can be answered with a simple "yes" or "no" response.

7. I play "Devil's Advocate" to help the other person see a different side of what they are saying.

8. If someone wants to talk about something over and over again, I'll just tell them what they want to hear to get them to stop.

9. As I listen, I am figuring out what I am going to say back to the other person.

10. I'm uncomfortable when people talk to me about sensitive subjects.

11. If another person has a different view on something I feel strongly about, I don't want to talk about it.

12. I don't really pay much attention to things like the environment or body language. What matters is what the other person is actually saying.

13. If the other person is struggling to say something, I'll fill in with my own suggestions.

14. If I'm interrupted from doing something when someone wants to talk, I feel impatient for them to finish so I can get back to what I was doing.

To determine your score, give yourself the following points for each answer:

Not at all = 1 point
Rarely = 2 points
Sometimes = 3 points
Often = 4 points
Very Often= 5 points

Score Interpretation

14–29 Gold Medalist You've got terrific listening skills already. You've got the ability to make people feel heard and want to talk to you. You're emotionally present and give people your full attention. But strive to continue to grow and evolve.

30–49 Silver Medalist People enjoy talking to you, but sometimes if subjects get too emotional or uncomfortable, you tend to change the subject or make a joke. The tools and ideas in this book will help you continue to grow and become a more effective listener.

50–70 The Bronze Medalist If you scored in this category, you might think you're a better listener than others do. You might be giving people the feeling that you don't care about what they're saying, or you might have frequent misunderstandings. Not to worry, though. The things you'll learn in this book can absolutely help you become a better listener.

Seven Types of Listeners

It was the quarterly "company wide" meeting, and the CEO started to suspect that some of the people on the video call weren't really listening to her.

Ben looked like he would rather be elsewhere, as he was looking away from the camera, down at his phone, and fidgeting.

Carolyn was completely zoned out. She was looking at the camera but had a totally blank look on her face.

As the CEO was explaining the reasoning behind the quarterly sales figures, David interjected, "A lot of it had to do with fuel prices, stemming from the conflict in the Middle East." He leaned back and smiled, and the CEO could see several others literally rolling their eyes at him.

Leah just muttered, "Whatever," so softly that barely anyone caught it.

Dan sat there with his arms crossed, frowning. "I don't mean to be rude, but couldn't this all have been an email? I don't know why we're wasting our time having a meeting about this."

"Actually, DAN, research shows that information that is presented using multiple modalities is more effectively absorbed than just reading an email." Margaret was practically glaring at her camera.

"I have a question for you?" Anna raised her hand. "We plan to release the new platform in the next quarter, right? How do these figures affect that rollout?"

How many times have you been talking and encountered someone like these meeting participants? How many times have you actually BEEN one of those listeners?

The above scenario illustrates the seven types of listeners identified by Dale Carnegie Training.

- The "Preoccupieds"
- The "Out-to-Lunchers"
- The "Interrupters"
- The "Whatevers"
- The "Combatives"
- The "Analysts"
- The "Engagers"

The first six types are less effective than the seventh. Here is a more in-depth description of each of the types.

The "Preoccupieds"

Ben was a classic "Preoccupied." Fidgeting and looking at the clock gives the speaker the impression that he isn't giving his full attention. These people come across as rushed and are constantly looking around or doing something else. Also known as multi-taskers, these people cannot sit still and listen.

The "Out-to-Lunchers"

In the above scenario, Carolyn was an "Out to Luncher." The CEO was talking, but she was daydreaming instead of listening. These people are physically there for you, but mentally, they are not. You can tell this by the blank look on their faces. They are either daydreaming or thinking about something else entirely.

The "Interrupters"

David is an "Interrupter." He was just waiting for his chance to jump in and speak. These people are ready to chime in at any given time. They are perched and ready for a break to complete your sentence for you. They are not listening to you. They are focused on trying to guess what you will say and what they want to say.

The "Whatevers"

Leah is a classic "Whatever." Even if she isn't actually using the word, her body language and demeanor gave the

CEO the feeling she didn't care about what he was saying at all. These people remain aloof and show little emotion when listening. They do not seem to care about anything you have to say.

The "Combatives"

It's pretty clear that Dan was a "Combative." Hostile and rude, the Combative listener isn't listening for understanding. He or she is listening to get ammunition to use against you. These people are armed and ready for war. They enjoy disagreeing and blaming others.

The "Analysts"

Margaret is an analyst. She probably has no idea that her listening style is ineffective. These people are constantly in the role of counselor or therapist, and they are ready to provide you with unsolicited answers. They think they are great listeners and love to help. They are constantly in an analyze-what-you-are-saying-and-fix-it mode.

The "Engagers"

Finally, Anna is an example of an "Engager." These are the consciously aware listeners. They listen with their eyes, ears, and hearts and try to put themselves in the speaker's shoes. This is listening at the highest level. Their listening skills encourage you to continue talking and give you the opportunity to discover your own solutions and let your ideas unfold.

Which type is most effective at building connections? In general, it's the latter, although there are times when the analysts skills are required and sought out. But until the solutions are asked for, it's better to focus on engaging.

No Time to Listen

Tom Mangan talks about a common misconception about listening. "Oftentimes people tell me that they don't have time to sit and listen to other people. 'I'm busy. I have things I need to be doing.'

"The resistance I often get in the leadership classes in particular is people saying, 'I don't have time for a conversation like that.' But it doesn't have to be a conversation. It can be simply just little touch points. It can take thirty seconds to two minutes to ask a question and listen for the answer.

"It's simply just shutting out the world and giving someone your undivided attention. We live in a world with screens and pop-ups and all these things competing for our attention. It's about making the other person feel valued and not like an inconvenience."

When we walk into someone's office, and they ask us "what is it," and then continue to type on their computer or stare at their phone, does that build the connections that we're trying to make? Almost always the answer is no. So let's not do that to other people.

No one can be an engaged listener all the time.

We talked earlier about open-ended questions. These are the types of questions that elicit responses and ask for more depth and insight from people. They encourage ideas and allow us to dig deeper into a topic to understand someone's perspective better. There are also closed-ended questions that are useful for closing down a discussion or moving on to another topic. Skilled listeners know that an ill-timed closed-ended question will shut down a valuable discussion, and that starting with them will lead to a short and invaluable discussion.

Open-ended questions:
• What is every idea you can imagine for solving this problem?
• What is your thinking?
• What are all of the types of food that you enjoy?
• Please tell me more about your experience

Closed-ended questions:
• Do you like this color?
• Is Chinese food your favorite?
• Does anyone have any questions?
• Does your dog bite?

> *"If you kNOw, there there's NO curiosity,*
> *there's NO learning, there's NO listening,*
> *there's NO connection"*
> —JONATHAN VEHAR

The Value of Humility

Research and experience working with leaders, great teams, people we like spending time with, and exceptional learners show that humility is at the foundation of many strengths, whether it is about being able to be coached, searching for new perspectives, listening effectively, tolerating ambiguity, or being open to new ideas. Humility is not something you do, it's a way of being. It's an on-going state of mind that requires us to constantly check-in to know if we're being an know-it-all (not attractive) or if we're recognizing that we don't know everything about the other person, which means that there's an opportunity to learn, empathize, and build a connection. People who demonstrate humility:

- Don't think they know everything, so they are curious, can learn, and from that make new potentially useful connections.
- Are easier to get along with than arrogant, so other people are more likely to want to connect with them.
- Don't need to get all of the credit, so others are willing to support them, as they know credit for accomplishment will be shared. This creates a sense of collaboration to create change and cooperation which makes our connections even stronger.

What's all this have to do with listening? Simple. When we are in a conversation as a "know-it-all," we're not really listening. When we come from an attitude of humility, we can be more clearly present because we're not trying to solve problems or jump in and share our brilliance. We're taking the opportunity to learn from the other person. When we're in a state of "not knowing," that's when we're really listening.

So that's the mindset for listening. Now here are some tools to help us in our listening.

The Listening Staircase

In our book *Listen!*, we shared a technique for becoming better at listening. We identified three types of questions that build on each other.

1. Elementary Questions

These questions determine basic information.

• What time is the next bus due to arrive?
• How much money is left in the budget?
• Is the cafeteria serving French fries today?

2. Elaborative Questions

Elaborate questions elaborate on the basic information we've already obtained.

• Do you know where the bus goes after the next stop?
• Is the money left in the budget allocated to anything in particular?
• What else is on the menu?

3. Evaluative Questions

These allow the other person to share their thoughts and opinions.

• Which musical acts would you love to see and hear perform live?

- I have some concerns about this strategy. What are some of the advantages to it?
- What improvements would you make to this product to help it sell better?

Also, in a previous chapter in this book, we explained that in the Innerview there are three types of questions:

1. Factual Questions

Questions of a typical conversational nature that revolve around factual information.

- Where did you grow up?
- Where did you go to school?
- How did the two of you meet?

2. Causative Questions

These questions determine the motive or causative factors behind some of the answers to the factual questions.

- What caused your parents to move there?
- Why did you pick that particular school?
- How did you come to work here?

3. Values-based Questions

These questions will allow you to better understand their frame.

- Tell me about a person who had a major impact on your life.
- If you had it to do over again, what would you do differently?
- What was the toughest part of your life? What got you through?

Now it's time to practice what we've learned. Using the following guide, determine what kind of questions follow. The answers are at the bottom of the page.*

A. "What time is the meeting?"
B. "How did you get a flat tire?"
C. "Do you prefer the blue or the red?"
D. "Why did you become a vegetarian?"
E. "What's the process for ordering replacement parts?"
F. "Which car gave you a smoother ride?"

____ Elementary
____ Evaluative
____ Elaborative
____ Factual
____ Causative
____ Values Based

The questions we ask come from and determine the frame by which we see the world. As we've learned, it's our frames and filters that create or prevent meaningful connections with others. In order to effectively listen, and get inside another person's frame, we've got to be able to ask meaningful and appropriate questions. When we combine these questioning skills with the conversation links (remember the nameplate on the dream house?), it allows us to dive deeper to create connections with substance and nuance.

David Kabakoff shares a story about how we can learn incredible things just by listening.

---

* A. Factual. B. Causative. C. Evaluative. D. Values Based. E. Elementary. F. Elaborative.

I was doing a workshop with eighty-five people in the room. There were two older gentlemen who'd known each other more than thirty years. Come to find out, they were both navy veterans who had been torpedoed down in the war and never knew this about each other!

Listening versus Empathetic Listening

Thus far in this chapter, we've talked about listening skills. These are the foundational skills that allow one to truly understand what another person is saying. In order to truly connect with that person, though, we must take it a step further than understanding. We've got to listen with empathy. But, what exactly is empathy?

Authors Larry Pate and Traci Shoblom, in a chapter published in *Organizing Through Empathy*, write, "According to the Perception Action Model, empathy is defined as a shared emotional experience occurring when one person (the subject) comes to feel a similar emotion to another (the object) as a result of perceiving the other's state. This process results from the fact that the subject's representations of the emotional state are automatically activated when the subject pays attention to the emotional state of the object."*

In other words, listening for understanding is one thing. Listening for empathy involves being able to emotionally

---

* Pate, L and Shoblom, T., "Organizing through empathy." (2015): 130–142

relate to the other person. This involves quieting the voices in our minds that say, "That's too bad that thing happened to you," for example, and reframing it with, "How would I feel if it happened to me?" Again, Dale Carnegie's 17th Principle says it this way, "Try honestly to see things from the other person's point of view."

Listen, Don't Just Hear

So the next time we're engaged in a conversation where we're looking to build, maintain, or rebuild a connection, let's focus on listening from the other person's perspective. Let's be deliberate about not just talking, but more importantly listening to hear what the other person is saying and where it's coming from inside of them.

The importance of being able to listen with the intention of learning and putting yourself in the shoes of another cannot be over-emphasized. The challenge is that most of us think we're great listeners. The reality is that we need to apply our humility, recognize that we can be better, and apply our tools to listen from the perspective of "not knowing." When we feel heard, we feel acknowledged, appreciated, and important. And that builds connections.

In this chapter, we talked about how being an effective empathetic listener requires humility and a willingness to be open to engaging with other people from their perspective. In the next chapter, we'll talk about how to do that when we don't have the benefit of being in their presence.

Key Takeaways

- There is a difference between Listening and Hearing. Listening means to actually understand and engage with the message.
- There are seven types of listeners. The "Engager" is the ideal type.
- Humility is important when listening. It's very easy to judge what the other person is saying as we are listening to them.
- There is a place for closed-ended questions (yes or no type) but to connect with others, use open ended questions.
- When asking questions, there are six types.
  —Elementary
  —Elaborative
  —Evaluative
  —Factual
  —Causative
  —Values-based
- These questions build on each other to form the Listening Staircase
- In order to truly connect with that person, though, we must take it a step further than understanding. We've got to listen with empathy.

9: VIRTUAL CONNECTIONS

"Hello? Are you there? I see your name but your mic and camera aren't on." Ernie absolutely hated virtual meetings. But in this day and age, there's no getting around them. "Maybe log off and then back on. See if that helps."

It's not that Ernie was uncomfortable with technology. He was in sales for a tech company, after all. It's that a large part of his work was forming relationships and connections with other people, and it was really hard to do when all you could see was their face on a screen in front of a virtual background. Many of the things he would normally use to build connections, such as personal items on a desk, weren't present in virtual meetings. Half the time, in large gatherings, people either had their cameras off, or they were clearly doing something else while attending the meeting.

There had to be a better way to connect with people when they weren't in the same room.

In the last chapter, we gave an example of a quarterly meeting conducted by a CEO that was virtual. More and more of us are finding ourselves in those kinds of meetings.

If in 2019 someone had told most of the people reading this book that we would all be wearing face masks and doing our work virtually for multiple years, we'd have thought they were crazy. But, of course, that's exactly what happened. Maybe the world was already moving in the direction of virtual workplaces, but the pandemic of 2020 definitely accelerated the era like a rocket sled! And it seems like that era is here to stay. With virtual reality workplaces emerging, and meetings being held by proxy with avatars and platforms such as Zoom, WebEx, and many others, we're all being required to learn new ways of interacting.

Frank Starkey shares an anecdote of how he learned to connect with others while wearing a face mask.

"When the pandemic started, we were all wearing masks. While doing so, I'm trying to smile through the mask by making my eyes really big. Imagine a person wearing a mask and since they can't smile with their mouth, they're making their eyes huge instead. I was creeping people out! Finally, I realized that it's not about making your eyes big, but it's about using your voice. Contrast this with my wife, who is the living embodiment of Dale Carnegie's principal number five: 'Smile.' I mean, she makes so many friends so easily because she's got this contagious smile. It goes all the way to her eyes. But me, I get my eyes going big and all you see are these big buggy eyes coming out from behind my mask. Right."

Frank's not alone. How many times did you try to smile at a stranger or a co-worker behind your mask only to realize that you were freaking them out because they couldn't see the smile and just thought you were staring at them.

Listening Without Words

If we are in a situation where we can't see the other person's full face (or in the case of virtual reality, we can't see them at all), how can we connect through listening? In another book in this series, *Listen!*, we talk about how to listen without words. It's about using non-verbal communication.

It's been said that—when there's conflict in what we're saying it and how we're saying it—only 7 percent of what we communicate is based on the words we speak, 38 percent of what we communicate is based on voice inflections, and 55 percent of what we communicate is based on non-verbal behavior. While the numbers may vary depending on the source, it's clear that we can do a lot of listening just by observing things other than a person's words.

In the scenario above, Frank made people uncomfortable by trying to make his eyes bigger. His wife made people more comfortable by smiling with her eyes ("Smizing").

Non-verbal communication is anything that communicates that is not a word.

Prior to people spending so much of our time on Zoom, we used the phone or email if we couldn't connect in person. Video-based conferencing opened up an entire new way of connecting, and like all new technologies, we're still adjusting to using it effectively and powerfully. Even those of us who have been using it for years. What video chat platforms have enabled is the ability to see (at least part) of the other person when we're connecting with them. While this provides some challenges like the so-called "Zoom fatigue," it also makes it possible for us to radically improve the quality of connection as opposed to speaking on the telephone or via email.

And of course with the opportunity to see the other person, it's important that we are doing that effectively to avoid misreading a situation and to ensure that we're building a strong connection.

Ten Cardinal Rules of Observation

In his book *What Every Body is Saying,* former FBI Agent and body language expert Joe Navarro gives Ten Cardinal Rules of Observation to use when you're listening to non-verbal communication.

1. You have to be a competent observer. This means you have to look around and observe the world around you constantly.
2. You have to observe all non-verbal communications in context. The context comes from the totality of what's going on in this person's life.
3. It's important to determine whether a behavior is coming from the brain or cultural.

4. Are the behaviors unique to this individual? Most people have certain behaviors that they engage in repeatedly.

5. If you're looking at non-verbal communications that are indicative of thoughts, feelings, or intentions, it's best to look for clusters of behaviors rather than relying on one thing.

6. Ask yourself, "What is normal behavior for this person or in this situation?"

7. Also ask yourself, "What behaviors are a change from normal?"

8. Focus on primacy. That is, look for the most immediate expressions as being the most accurate, and using that information as you analyze non-verbal communication.

9. The observations that we make should be non-intrusive.

10. Any time you see a behavior, if you're not sure what it means, always divide it up into one of two columns. Does it fit within comfort, or does it fit within discomfort? It's either going to be a comfort display, or a discomfort display.

Body Talk

Because such a huge part of listening involves observing non-verbal signals, it's helpful to know what to notice. Again, it's important to take these items within the context of the Ten Cardinal Rules.

Here are some interesting things you can look for to tell when someone is comfortable or uncomfortable in their communication with you when you can't see their whole body.* Use these signals when you're building connections with others, and be aware of what you're unintentionally signaling to others through your body language.

Arms

One of the truly powerful ways that we use our hips is what's called arms akimbo. Most of the time, when you see someone standing there with their hands on their hips, elbows out, their legs are slightly spread apart, this is a very territorial display. This is what we see when someone is in charge, when someone's in command. It's a very commanding presence. It can also indicate a problem with the situation. Although we can't see full Arms Akimbo when we can't see someone's lower body, we can see a version of this when they prop their arms up on a desk in a commanding position.

Crossing of the arms can have both a positive connotation and a negative one. To determine which it is, you have to look at the grip. When people are talking to each other and their arms are crossed, but they're gripping their arms very tightly, it's usually indicative of something very negative.

Otherwise, it doesn't necessarily associate with something negative. One can have their arms crossed, leaning back on a chair, and be very relaxed. When we are in a social setting where there are other people around us, we derive a certain amount of comfort putting our hands across our chest and so forth.

---

* These are derived from Joe Navarro's book, *What Every Body is Saying*

At times when we want to create a psychological barrier, we'll place an object like a pillow or a blanket or a coat over our arms or torso.

Hands

The hands are one of the best places to look for non-verbal messages. When we put our fingers together, the thumb and the first two fingers, we can indicate precision. We can talk about something expansive by using jazz hands where we extend our fingers fully and they stretch, and we are transported to something differently when we use expressive hands. You'll note that politicians do this a lot.

Steepling is when we bring our fingertips together, but don't allow our palms to touch, so that our fingers look like a church steeple. Steepling is in fact the most powerful behavior that we have to show confidence. It shows that we're very confident about what we're talking about.

Shoulders

Imagine a teenager being asked the question, "Is your brother home from school yet?" She brings one shoulder up to the ear and says, "I don't know." Now, contrast that with her being asked, "Is your brother home from school yet?", but both shoulders come up to the ears, her palms up, and she says, "I don't know." Which is more believable? When someone is hunching their shoulders or shrugging, they're not sure of what they are saying or what they are hearing. Shoulders back can indicate confidence, leaning forward can indicate interest.

Neck

The neck is one of those places where we tend to touch to soothe ourselves when we are under stress. Massaging the back of the neck while speaking is a classic indicator of discomfort.

When women feel insecure, when they're distressed, when they're troubled or they feel threatened, they'll cover this little area called the supra sternal notch—this neck dimple—with the tips of their fingers, or with their hands.

Head

This is another area where you can observe if someone is listening to you or convey to someone that you're listening to them. You're talking to someone, and at some point in the conversation, your head begins to comfortably tilt as you're listening to them. If something is mentioned that you don't particularly care for, your head will immediately straighten up.

Forehead

The forehead is one of the easiest places on the body to determine anxiety. The forehead is one of those areas of the bodies that, in real-time, presents us with a very accurate picture as to a person's thoughts and feelings. It very easily, very clearly can show us when there is stress, when there is comfort, when things are not going the right way, or when something is trouble us.

Eyes

While most people think of blinking the eyes as merely a way to lubricate them, it's actually a very effective blocking mechanism. Most of the time, when we hear something we don't like, we actually close our eyes. Sometimes it's just for a tenth of a second, sometimes it's for a little longer, but one of the ways that the human brain found to protect itself is to use this blocking mechanism.

Many times when we hear bad news, or we are being told of something that stresses us, you'll find yourself closing your eyes as you are processing this information. So, if someone is listening to you, and they close their eyes, it might not be that they aren't listening. It might be that they don't like what you're telling them.

Eyebrows

This is one of the classic comical gestures to indicate interest. A man looks at a woman, nods his head, and his eyebrows go up, as if to say, "How YOU doin'?" This is called the Eyebrow Flash, and is a sign of comfort or interest.

Imagine meeting someone and, as you go to shake their hand, their eyes are just fixed, and then you meet another person and as you go to shake their hand, they look at you and they arch their eyebrows in what's known as the eyebrow flash.

Mouth

When we have a true, sincere smile, the muscles around the eyes are engaged in the process. In a true smile, the corners of the mouth come up towards the eyes and the eyes will reflect that, because the muscles of the eyes will be involved in that smile. Sadly, this is where we get the "crow's feet" effect.

The false smile—the social smile—is the smile that moves the corners of the mouth towards the ears, but does not involve the eyes. This is one of the ways that we assess for genuine emotions. The lips can disappear because of the high degree of stress that the person is undergoing. It has nothing to do with deception. It has nothing to do with truth or lying. When you see lips that have disappeared, there's a high degree of stress. Lip tension is mental tension and when the corners of the mouth turn downward then emotions are really low.

Biting the lip and cheek can have different connotations as well. This is why it's so important to keep these observations in context. For example, George W. Bush used to bite the inside of his cheek when he is highly nervous or anxious, and Bill Clinton had a tendency to bite his lower lip as a way of demonstrating his sincerity.

Chin

We've all seen the classic professor or therapist move—touching the chin or stroking a beard (real or imaginary). Chin touching is associated with pensiveness, with thinking, with thought, and with precision of ideas.

Now, this is to be differentiated from people who touch their face, especially around the jaw line. We tend to pacify ourselves by touching our jaws, and then we tend to show we're thinking of something by touching this little very narrow area that is about two inches wide on our chin.

The jaw can also tell us about confidence or insecurity. When we're strong and confident, our jaw comes out. When we are weak and insecure, and when we lack confidence, we tuck our chin in.

Preening

We see it all over the animal kingdom. Animals "preen" as an effort to make themselves look attractive to the opposite sex. Humans are animals too but instead of fluffing our feathers, we adjust our hair, glasses, jewelry, or straighten our ties.

Preening in this manner sends a very powerful message to the other people who are in your presence. It subconsciously conveys to them, "You're important enough for me to spend this energy to put myself together to preen for you." There are also negative preening behaviors too. We see it in movies. A bad guy is trying to intimidate someone, and he's talking to him, and start picking lint off the other person's clothes or adjusts his glasses. It's a sign of disrespect, and when the other person allows it to continue, it's a strong statement of not having power in the situation.

Pacifying

We tend to think of pacifying as something that babies do to calm themselves down, such as sucking their thumb or twirling their hair. Although we do see it in young children, pacifying behaviors continue on in adulthood as well.

Here are some examples. When you see a person doing this, it means that they are feeling anxious.

- Rubbing their forehead
- Pulling on their hair
- Rubbing their nose
- Massaging their nose
- Pulling on their upper lip
- Stroking their chin
- Massaging their ears
- Pulling on their earlobes
- Twirling a pencil
- Mangling a paperclip
- Playing with a rubber band
- Rubbing their fingers
- Playing with jewelry (twisting a ring or pulling on a necklace)

Recognize that we don't mean to suggest that these are always true, or that you should memorize and interpret them at face-value. In fact, we may be sending multiple conflicting signals. To build connections, we might ask the other person about the behavior in order to get clarification.

Cam Robertson notes that for years he's received feedback that when he's thinking, he looks angry. "Yes! I furrow my brow when I'm concentrating on something or thinking about an issue through. I've had bosses and colleagues ask me, 'are you angry about something?' And I explain to them that it's my RTF. My Resting Thinking Face, and it only means that I'm thinking or concentrating. When I notice myself doing it—and spending hours and hours on

Zoom has helped me work on this—I intentionally relax my eyebrows and raise them slightly to convey interest and not anger."

Using Non-Verbal Communication to Convey Listening

Much of what we've covered here is how we can use observations of non-verbal communication to listen to what a speaker is saying, beyond words.

But you can also use it to let the other person know that you are listening to them.

When listening, you can use non-verbal communication to SOFTEN the position of others:

S = Smile
O = Open posture
F = Forward lean
T = Touch
E = Eye contact
N = Nod

Using Non-Verbal Signals

Perhaps the best use of non-verbal signals in the virtual setting is to bring them out in the open to start an honest dialogue. The other person is giving us clues to how they are really feeling, and we can use that information to "make it about the other person."

It can look something like this, "I am sensing that you don't agree with what I'm saying." Or, "You look stressed out. How are things going for you today?" These kinds of bridges lead to deeper connections, despite the fact that we may be halfway across the world from each other.

Grace Dagres shares a story about how she makes connections in a virtual world.

"Even when I'm on a Zoom call, I'm trying to remember 'It's not about me.' What does the other person want to talk about? What do they want to hear about what's helpful for them? Because I can talk to my family all day long about what I want. So it's about finding out what they want to talk about and then finding commonality. But you have to be careful not to take the conversation back. For example, when my son was in high school, he played football and they had a state championship winning team. They won several state championships. And so if I was talking to somebody and they said, and they said, 'Oh, you know, our son plays high school football,' I'm going to be tempted to tell them all about my son and his team. Instead, all I say is, 'Really? So does my son!' And then you stop. Let the other person keep talking.

"So whether you're in person, you're on Zoom or any other environment you're in, it doesn't matter how comfortable we are. It doesn't. It's not about us. It's about making the other person feel comfortable. Because if they're not comfortable, you're not gonna make a connection."

Helping Others Connect Virtually

Tom Mangan shares some advice on how to help other people connect virtually. It comes from the questions we ask to learn about other people and then making mental connections about things others might have in common.

"We think, 'Oh, I'm talking to Bill. I know Bill but you don't. Actually, Bill knows this person who knows this other person. It's six degrees of separation. But if you never ask enough questions to find out that Bill had his first job in a yogurt shop and that Mark's daughter works at a yogurt shop now, we won't have anything to grab on to.

"That's one of the reasons that I really like social media is because they point out these connections. Several years ago, there were these two dogs going through the neighborhood because they'd gotten out. So, I got the dogs and put them in my fenced in yard. I then went onto the Next-Door social media platform and posted, 'Hey if anyone is missing their dogs, I have them.' Now, the surprising thing was that I got a response from a guy in Germany who didn't even live in our neighborhood any more. 'Those dogs live at the blue house on the next block.'"

Social media often gets a bad rap, and when we see someone looking down at their phones we tend to assume that they're disengaged, when in fact they might just be making virtual connections. Like most things, social media is neither good nor bad. However, like most tools, it can be used badly or abused. When used properly it can be useful to make connections using all of the principles we've talked about in this book.

What about when we don't need to meet virtually or face-to-face? Pilgrimage Professional Development Group lists five reasons to meet:

1. To inform
2. To explore
3. To debate
4. To decide
5. To connect

Before we agree to meet, it's important to be clear on what we're meeting about, and whether or not we can do it with an email, phone call, or text. And notice that the last reason to get together is to connect. It's a powerful drive that is critical for getting things done, whether we're trying to do it by ourselves or with others.

Email and Text

An overlooked way to connect with others (and help others connect with each other) is through email and text. With written communication, we don't get the benefit of non-verbal cues, and things can often be misconstrued because we can't hear tone when we're reading.

A "warm" introduction, whether it's of yourself, or another, can go a long way to creating a connection.

Here are some tips for connecting with others through writing.

- Be specific. Use specific information that you know about the person to create a connection. "I grew up in a snowy climate. I bet you're ready for Spring!"
- Be friendly. An introductory email should set the recipient at ease. This isn't the time to be critical of another person.

- Be respectful. It is very easy for things to be misunderstood, so be extra careful that what you say cannot be taken another way.
- Spell their name right! There are very few worse things than getting someone's name wrong. If it's Terri with an "i," don't write Terry. It diminishes your credibility.
- Ask questions to show your interest. This isn't the place for lengthy exposition about your opinions or history. Instead, ask the other person for their thoughts.
- Be clear. It's easy to get caught up in trying to dash off a note, and in trying to be brief, we don't properly convey what we want. While brevity is important, so is clarity. Take time to articulate what's necessary for people to take action.
- Put yourself in the reader's place. Once we've written it, imagine we're the reader sitting in front of the message, and knowing what they know and what they want to know, have we been clear? Have we covered what we need to? Have we clearly articulated why this message is relevant to them and what we're expecting of them as a result of this note?

Suggestions for Connecting Virtually

Just as Part One of this book covered the things that we can do ourselves to get in the right mindset for connection, thus far this chapter has talked about how we can convey and interpret information virtually. As we learned in the chapter on listening, true connection goes deeper than skills. Connecting virtually is about more than watching one's body language or observing others. It's about finding out how we can connect virtually at the same emotional level as if we were face-to face.

Here are some suggestions on how to create an emotional connection virtually. (You'll notice that they are quite similar to how we create emotional connections in person.)

• Set an intent for connection. This means, before you even go into the virtual setting, decide that you will form connections with the others in the room. Instead of putting off that weekly team meeting, look at it as a way to connect with others whom you might not get a chance to meet otherwise.

• Listen more than you speak. It's so easy, especially in a virtual setting, to decide what our response will be and then tune out until it's our turn to speak. Instead, dig deeper and keep listening. Look at the body language of the speaker and see what you observe. Is he or she nervous? Proud? Shy? Use that emotion to create a connection when you DO speak. "I just want to commend Amy for speaking up here. It can be nerve-wracking to say something so controversial."

• Use private messages in group chats to communicate one on one. Ask how someone's day is going or what they think of the new company logo.

• Share something (moderately) personal. Earlier in the book we explored how disclosing something moderately personal creates a sense of connection between two people. "My Great Dane puppy destroyed my couch last month."

- Get proactive! Start a virtual club, lunch, message thread, competition, or some other way to engage with people virtually.
- Act normal. This might sound like odd advice, but sometimes we're so concerned with how we look on camera that we get stiff or overly formal. Instead, smile, look at the camera when speaking, and realize that everyone else also thinks they look horrible on camera too.
- Be willing to be a little vulnerable. If we're on the call and we're having trouble understanding something because it's unclear or maybe audio dropped out, let's ask the question. Likely we'll be serving the group needs in the process and that will make us more relatable.
- Practice the pause. When we're in person and we ask a question, usually someone will answer within three seconds if we wait that long (most people don't, and immediately answer their own question). When virtual, it takes much longer to get responses. Because it's harder to read the social cues, and we have to take ourselves off mute, and because we're being polite so that others can speak first, and for other reasons, it just takes longer for answers and discussion to start. Let's get into the practice of counting to ten or even fifteen once we ask a question to get a response from the group.

The bottom line is that connecting virtually is basically the same as connecting in person. All of the ideas and techniques we covered in this book apply just as well virtually as they do when we are face-to-face.

Key Takeaways

- If we are in a situation where we can't see the other person's full face (or in the case of virtual reality, we can't see them at all) we have to become astute at other ways of connecting. It starts with observing non-verbal behavior
- Ten Rules of observation
    1. Be a competent observer
    2. Observe all non-verbal communications in context
    3. Determine whether a behavior is coming from the brain or cultural
    4. Identify if the behaviors are unique to the individual
    5. Look for clusters of behaviors
    6. Ask if the behavior is normal
    7. Ask if the behaviors are a change from normal
    8. Focus on the most immediate expressions
    9. Don't be intrusive
    10. Are the behaviors based on comfort or discomfort?
- Here are some ways to nonverbally convey listening. It's the acronym SOFTEN:
    S = Smile
    O = Open posture
    F = Forward lean
    T = Touch
    E = Eye contact
    N = Nod

- Connecting virtually is about more than watching one's body language or observing others. It's about finding out how we can connect virtually at the same emotional level as if we were face-to face.
- The best way to connect virtually is the same way we connect non-virtually. Be humble, be authentic, and "it's not about you."

CONCLUSION: Dale Carnegie Principles for Connection

Humans crave connections. Fundamentally, it is the basis of our relationships, our work, and society. Surgeon Paul Brand once described a lecture given by the prominent anthropologist Margaret Mead.* "To her, evidence of the earliest true civilization was a healed femur, a leg bone, which she held up before us in the lecture hall. She explained that such healings were never found in the remains of competitive, savage societies. There, clues of violence abounded: temples pierced by arrows, skulls crushed by clubs. But the healed femur showed that someone must have cared for the injured person—hunted on his behalf, brought him food, and served him at personal sacrifice."

---

* 1980 Copyright, Fearfully and Wonderfully Made: A Surgeon Looks at the Human and Spiritual Body by Dr. Paul Brand and Philip Yancey, Chapter: Bones: A Frame, Quote Page 68, Zondervan Publishing House, Grand Rapids, Michigan. Cited on https://quoteinvestigator.com/2021/07/25/femur/#f+439945+1+1

Yes, connection. This primitive man survived because of connection.

As we've mentioned throughout this, and the other four books in this series, the principles that Dale Carnegie set forth in his books are as practical and relevant today as they were then. You can literally flip open *How to Win Friends and Influence People* and read a passage and discover that it applies to a situation you are currently in. This is true whether you're building connections face-to-face or virtually. In real time or asynchronously.

In order to make meaningful, trust-based connections with others, we must form a habit of applying Dale Carnegie's principles. We must apply them ourselves, inspire others to achieve similar results, and become a champion of these concepts.

Doing so will, no exaggeration, make our world a better place for everyone. These connections will help us develop personal confidence to deal with others, reduce our anxiety, allow for better communication between individuals and groups, reduce conflict, increase productivity and efficiency, and best of all, create deep, lasting emotional bonds with others. It helps us, and it helps make the world we share better.

> *"The rare person who tries to unselfishly*
> *serve others has an enormous advantage."*
> Dale Carnegie

APPENDIX:

Excerpts from the other books in the Dale Carnegie Training series: *Listen!, Sell!, Lead!, Speak!*

LISTEN!

The Art of Effective Communication

INTRODUCTION

*And so I had him thinking of me as a good
conversationalist when, in reality, I had been merely
a good listener and had encouraged him to talk.*
—DALE CARNEGIE

The Dilemma of the Orange*

Two teenagers were having an argument. They both wanted an orange, but there was only one left.

"I want it!"

"No, I do!"

Their mother heard them arguing and went to see what was going on. "How about you split it?"

---

* This story comes from conflict management professor Dr. Alan Filley.

They both asserted, "No! I need the whole orange."

They were devising all kinds of "fair" ways to see who would get the orange. Rock, paper, scissors. Flipping a coin. Drawing straws. But they couldn't agree on how to decide who should get the orange.

After listening to all of this, their mother said, "Well, what do you need the orange for?"

"I need the juice for my smoothie."

"I need the rind for my cake."

Suddenly the teenagers looked at each other and started laughing. They each could have the whole orange! One would take the juice, and the other would take the rind. It took their mother asking the right question and their listening to the answer to solve what seemed like an impossible dilemma.

The Art of Listening

How many times has this happened to you? Two people have conflicting needs, and it seems as if the only solution is that one person won't get their needs met. It happens all the time at work, at home, and in family and professional relationships.

What if there were a way to think differently? A way that smoothed conflict, built stronger relationships, and allowed you to step back and see the bigger picture? What if there were a way to make all of your relationships better? There is. It's called *listening*.

There is a way to make your relationships better. It's called listening.

Listening alone won't cut it. It's not about sitting by and passively saying, "Uh huh. And how does that make you feel?" while mentally preparing your response. You have to know the right questions to ask, how to listen effectively, and what to do once you've gained understanding. It's about really stepping into another person's reality and seeing how they view the world.

Effective listening isn't something that comes naturally. No one is born with it. You don't see a toddler going, "So, Jimmy, what do YOU need the orange for?" Effective listening is really a learned art. After all, what is art but the practice of creation? When you actually listen to what another person is saying—not just their words, but the entire context of the communication—you create a relationship with that person. The relationship may last five minutes or fifty years. The truth is, communication creates—or destroys—relationships.

That's why Dale Carnegie Training has written this book. Although effective listening is an art, it's also a skill. Just as a painter or a sculptor masters his or her craft by learning, practicing, and repeating, you can learn to become a more effective listener. When you do, you'll find that a whole world will open up to you that you may not have seen before. A world where you can figure out what a person is really trying to say, not just what the words are conveying.

One where you can manage anger and uncomfortable emotions during conversation and avoid escalating arguments. You'll discover how to listen so that the other person feels heard and is more likely to be able to hear you as well. With *Listen!,* you, too, can master the art of communication.

SELL!

The Way Your Customers Want to Buy

DALE CARNEGIE:
THE NEW GENERATION

(And Why You Should Read This Book!)

New York City, 1912

In the same year that the Titanic hit the iceberg, Dale Carnegie began teaching lessons in public speaking at the YMCA in New York City's Harlem district. He had persuaded the YMCA manager to allow him to instruct a class in return for 80 percent of the net proceeds.* Dale Carnegie had begun what would evolve into his classic human-relations course. The far-reaching success of his

---

* "Dale Carnegie Discovered 'How to Win Friends and Influence People' in Harlem, 1911," *Harlem World* website, Nov. 26, 2017: https://www.harlemworldmagazine.com/dale-carnegie-discovered-win-friends-influence-people-harlem-1911.

training ultimately led him to publish *How to Win Friends and Influence People* in 1936. Carnegie believed that if he could "help people realize their own unsuspected powers," he would not have lived in vain.

Clearly that was a long time ago. A lot in our world has changed. But there are just as many things that haven't changed. Dale Carnegie launched an entire personal-development industry and changed the way business books were written.

In fact, *How to Win Friends and Influence People* continues to be a best-seller, ranking as the eleventh best-selling book on Amazon of all time. Why is that? Why, in a world where there are 52 million books for sale on Amazon, does Dale Carnegie's classic stay fresh?

It's because some things never go out of fashion. Things like admitting when you're wrong, striving to make a good impression, and giving effective feedback are timeless ideas that need to be passed down from generation to generation. Human nature hasn't changed, nor have the principles for building trust, communicating effectively, and influencing and leading people. Carnegie's principles are timeless, and his formulas for leading an intentional, mindful, and successful life continue to be passed down from generation to generation.

Today Dale Carnegie's legacy is as strong as ever. With a roster of more than 8 million graduates, Dale Carnegie's 2000 professional trainers are passionately committed to unlocking the inherent potential of individuals, teams, and organizations in more than eighty-five countries and thirty languages.

New York City, late 2018

When I first started my career, I had always known I wanted to do something that was relationship-driven. I first started in an account-management and customer-success role at the audio company Audible. I would work with customers after the contract was signed. I would make sure that they had everything they needed and that all problems were fixed or addressed. Eventually I was asked to take on more of a sales-hunting role in addition to the account management I was currently doing.

This was a bit scary for me for a few reasons. For one thing, public speaking absolutely terrified me. I would take those classes in college, get up in front of everyone, and completely freeze, and with sales there's a lot of addressing groups of people. It's giving your pitches and PowerPoint presentations and convincing potential clients about something they either need or want.

Second, I had always pictured salespeople as not being fully authentic or transparent. I didn't want to go into something where my quota, while important, meant putting customers second and pressuring them into buying something that wasn't right for them, knowing that eventually it would result in an angry customer—someone who would not stay around for the long run.

After a bit of thought, I decided to see what courses were out there to help me. I had heard of Dale Carnegie before, and after reading the reviews decided to find their sales course. I ended up choosing a three-day course in New York City, and decided this was the next step to figuring out if sales would be the right path for me.

As I was walking to class the first day, I remember being nervous. I thought I was going to be surrounded by salespeople who had been in the business for years. I didn't want to be the kid in class getting eye rolls because I was asking silly questions. I also had tons of questions running through my head: Is sales the direction my life is going to go in? Am I going to take this class and then reevaluate my entire career? Is Dale Carnegie going to turn me into a smooth-talking salesperson who can get anyone to buy anything at any cost?

After arriving in the classroom and talking with people, I had realized I had built up the people joining the class to be like the sharks from *Shark Tank*, but fortunately that wasn't the reality of the situation at all. I sat down with a group of great people; all of them were from different industries, with all types of sales experience.

Throughout the three days, my confidence in my sales skills boomed. I went from someone who thought I could never go into sales because it just wasn't me as a person to someone who was excited to go back to my company and take on this new challenge.

One of the points in Dale Carnegie's golden book to win people to your way of thinking is Principle 20: "Dramatize Your Ideas." This changed the way I sold. A few weeks after the class, I was working with a potential customer; after hearing all about their pain points, I knew my product was perfect for them. Through what I learned in my course, I was able to paint a picture for them of how my product would fix the pain points they had mentioned. Not only did this get them excited, but they increased the size of the deal, making them our largest client at the time.

I left Dale Carnegie not only knowing I wanted to go into sales but with a passion to take over the sales world. I went back to my company, ended up adding sales hunting to my résumé and within the first six months I was the top sales performer on the team and was promoted to sales manager.

Dale Carnegie helped me fine-tune my relationship skills, but also helped me put my passion for the products I sell into words in order to make others passionate as well. My Golden Book trophy has been on my desk since the day I won that challenge. It's a reminder to remember that I can be authentic and transparent while being a good salesperson, and for that I'll be eternally thankful.

—Samantha Finan*

---

* Samantha (Finan) Pavlik is, as of this writing, an Account Executive at LinkedIn Marketing Solutions

LEAD!

How to Build a High-Performing Team

INTRODUCTION

Blending Performance Needs with Human Needs

It was pitch black and the sound of falling rocks could still be heard. It was every miner's nightmare. In a matter of minutes that sound meant that the nightmare had become reality for thirty-four men trapped below the surface of the earth in Chile in 2010. Foreman Luis Urzua knew at that moment that the only way to keep himself and the other trapped miners alive was to rapidly develop a plan that would keep them safe until help could arrive, and provide realistic hope that they would survive despite the terrifying situation.

Within moments of the collapse, Luis gathered the men together and began formulating. They developed a three-pronged strategy with three goals in mind. Keep the men healthy and alive, create order and structure while they waited, and work with the rescuers to give them the information they needed. He knew that he needed to oversee, protect, and balance the physical, emotional, and human needs of thirty-four people, potentially for months.

To accomplish the physical goal of *sustaining life*, Luis implemented a strict food rationing system—each person received two spoonfuls of tuna and half a glass of milk every other day. This kept them alive until the rescuers were able to pass food down through a small hole drilled into the earth.

To *create order and structure*, Luis led the men to organize different living spaces underground. Using his skills as a topographer, he divided the area into a work area, a sleeping space, and other defined areas. He created an artificial "day" and "night" by using the headlights of trucks in the mine to simulate daylight.

To *keep safe*, the men worked to chip away at the "roof" so that rocks wouldn't fall on them at night. And to *assist in their rescue*, they drew sophisticated maps of the underground and passed them up to rescue workers.

In addition to tending to the physical needs of the group, he also created a "leadership team" designating men to fill roles as a medic, a chaplain, and someone to administer the medical and psychological tests being sent from the surface to monitor their mental and emotional health.

For almost two months, the men lived, worked, and celebrated the small wins achieved daily.

In the end, the men were rescued after 70 days, with Luis being the last man out. Every single person lived, and they all attributed this to Luis Urzua's emergent leadership skills.

While this example is an extreme case of life or death, the leadership lessons we can draw from it apply in many different circumstances.

None of us have been trapped in a cave for almost two months in the dark. But many of us have had the experience of hearing rumors of a merger, a "restructuring," a layoff, or closure that no one in upper management can confirm or deny. What do we do when we have a team of people looking at us for guidance, but we're "in the dark," too?

Or when our boss is suddenly let go or quits and there's a huge gap in the organizational structure. Now it's up to us to lead, even though we may not be formally in that role. It's fairly easy to be an empathetic, trustworthy leader when things are going well—but what about when they're not? When there's chaos and uncertainty, the best intentions of leaders sometimes disappear. That's true for leaders around us and for ourselves.

At its core, leadership is a way to achieve results through and with other people. The results may look different from organization to organization, and the people and methods may change, but the fundamental requirements of a leader are the same. Leaders have to focus on engaging people or teams of people, balancing competing priorities, defining and communicating direction in a way that inspires and compels, and using the resources on hand to their full potential.

The leader isn't always the one out front waving the flag, with the band marching behind her. Leadership isn't about who gets credit for the work, or doing the work one's self, or looking good to customers or other stakeholders. True leadership is about *gaining willing cooperation about where to go and how to get there, and then using patience and skill to motivate and guide everyone there.*

Leadership can be designated ("congratulations, you've been promoted!"), or can emerge naturally from within a group ("we value that you've got such great experience and/or insights"). It can be situationally dependent ("you're the only one with experience with this new system"), or can be role-related ("you're leading the team as part of your job"). But in every case, the leader has to be on his or her toes to handle the variability of change. People are different and are not consistent, resources come and go, and the amount of information we have at any given time is in flux.

The day that Luis Urzua went to work before the collapse, he had no idea how quickly everything would change. Fortunately, he had a core set of leadership skills, values, and principles that let him respond quickly to an emergency. And he was willing to step up and take on the burden of leadership (in this case knowing that the group depended upon his leadership for their very survival) when he could have broken down and waited for someone else to do something.

At Dale Carnegie Training we've seen leaders from all walks of life demonstrate incredible leadership skills like these in all kinds of situations. Never has it been more evident than during the recent pandemic. Leaders had to flex with ongoing uncertainty, while juggling the demands of protecting people and the bottom line. In many cases, we had to learn how to manage a remote team of people who had no idea how to work remotely. Leadership is enough of a challenge without the methods of interacting changing practically overnight.

Why put in the hard work? Because leaders impact the lives of their followers, as well as the whole culture in which they operate. From small "mom and pop" businesses to global corporations, the relationship that the leader has with his or her people makes the difference between success and failure in a company.

SPEAK!

How to Get Over the Fear and Horror of Public Speaking

INTRODUCTION

Mark Cahill* sat in the outer office of an upscale office building in New York City and was waiting to be called in to give the presentation of his career. He'd been working as a sales person for this particular large, multinational company, and was a subject matter expert on a specific piece of equipment that the company was thinking of selling internationally. If the presentation went well, it would surely mean a promotion and a raise—as well as a massive career boost.

"They're ready for you, Mr. Cahill," the receptionist said as she opened the double glass doors.

---

* All of the names and identifying company information in this book have been changed, unless specific permission has been given to use it.

As he stood up to follow her in, Mark thought he might throw up. His head got light and all he could hear were the voices of doubt in his head. "What makes you think you'll have anything interesting to say? Don't you remember that speech class you took in high school? They literally laughed at you."

"Mr. Cahill?" The woman stood at the door, looking at him expectantly.

"Well, I can't get out of it now," Mark thought as he swallowed his nerves and headed into the conference room where the executive team sat waiting for him. "Let's get this over with."

Mark is not alone in his fear of public speaking. Research shows that as much as 77% of people around the world have some level of fear when it comes to speaking in front of others. Publicspeaking is one of the most fear-evoking events on the planet. In *SPEAK!: Getting Over the Fear and Horror of Public Speaking* we'll discover that there's no need to worry, because "it's not about the speaker, it's about the message and the audience." What this means is that one doesn't need to become some "polished professional speaker," and instead can reflect their authentic true self. Rather than focusing on being a good speaker, as Dale Carnegie put it, "Be a good person, speaking."

Our impact as a speaker comes from who we are as a person. What this means is that what makes YOU a good speaker is going to be different than what makes your neighbor, your coworker, or your sister a good speaker. So we need to stop trying to mimic our favorite great speaker (we're not them, and they're not us). Instead we must be the best person that we can be. When we do that, we'll influence our audiences.

This book reflects Dale Carnegie's thinking and what is taught in his High Impact Presentation course. It is based on the timeless principles contained in his book *How to Win Friends and Influence People.* The stories you'll read are true, and the tips we share come from those who have mastered the art of public speaking: our best trainers around the world.

Why Public Speaking?

There are many ways to change the world and to make an impact around us. Yet nothing works without the ability to influence people, and that is the role of public speaking.

When we think of "public speaking," we envision a politician or motivational speaker up on a stage in front of throngs of people in an audience. While that is one form of public speaking, it's unlikely that any of us "regular folks" will find ourselves speaking to hundreds, thousands or even tens of thousands of people. More likely, "public speaking" will take the form of a work presentation, a speech to a group we belong to, standing up in a house of worship, or even a toast at a family member's wedding, or even a one-on-one with a customer, client or boss. In each of these settings, we are addressing a group of people with a desire to impact them in some way. We might be trying to persuade the group to invest, or to present some findings or figures. Or, we might want to honor, entertain, emotionally move, or inspire the audience. Whatever the outcome, public speaking is how we impact and change the world.

*   *   *

Classic Advice Doesn't Cut It Anymore

When we think back on some of the advice given to help public speakers "get over" their fear, some of it is downright absurd. Have you heard any of these "classic" tips?
• Imagine the audience in their underwear
• Stare at a point on the wall just over the audience's heads
• Write your key phrases on the palm of your hand
• Crack a joke to break the ice
• Pace around the stage to generate energy

This is the kind of advice that used to be given to new speakers learning to get over their fear of public speaking.

There's nothing wrong, necessarily, with wearing new clothes to a talk (unless you're trying to break in new shoes). It's that these tips, and most advice we hear, is about YOU, the speaker.

At Dale Carnegie, the most consistent piece of advice we give to people learning to improve their speaking skills is completely the opposite of this. We teach, as Clark Merrill says, "It's not about you. It's about the audience." When we focus on the message the audience needs to hear, and how it will be received by the audience, the fear of speaking dissipates. We're no longer worried about what they think of us (is my tie straight, do I have lipstick on my teeth, I hate my speaking voice, am I moving my hands correctly, et cetera). Instead, we are able to turn that energy outward and connect with the audience by being our true selves.

The Trust Formula

When we're speaking to an audience, whether it's large or small, we're trying to create trust in the room—trust in what we're saying, trust in the audience, trust in the speaker. In order to create trust, we need to demonstrate credibility and empathy.

$$\text{Trust} = \text{Credibility} + \text{Empathy}$$

Credibility is about getting the audience to believe us. It's about earning the right to speak to them, and then defeating any doubts they might have. They must believe in us and our ability to lead them through the presentation, otherwise they won't be willing to be engaged or have their thinking shaped by what we have to say. We can't do that by being something or someone we're not.

INDEX

CPSIA information can be obtained
at www.ICGtesting.com
Printed in the USA
JSHW051601120722
27879JS00001B/2